AF352541

SPEAKING TRUTH TO POWER

Speaking Truth to Power

The Legacy of the Young Cid

MATTHEW BAILEY

UNIVERSITY OF TORONTO PRESS
Toronto Buffalo London

ISBN 978-1-4875-0687-2 (cloth) ISBN 978-1-4875-3507-0 (EPUB)
ISBN 978-1-4875-3506-3 (PDF)

Library and Archives Canada Cataloguing in Publication

Title: Speaking truth to power : the legacy of
the young Cid / Matthew Bailey.
Names: Bailey, Matthew, 1955– author.
Series: Toronto Iberic.
Description: Series statement: Toronto Iberic |
Includes bibliographical references.
Identifiers: Canadiana (print) 20230442692 | Canadiana (ebook) 20230442706 |
ISBN 9781487506872 (cloth) | ISBN 9781487535070 (EPUB) |
ISBN 9781487535063 (PDF)
Subjects: LCSH: Crónica rimada del Cid – Criticism, Textual. |
LCSH: Cid, approximately 1043–1099. | LCSH: Epic poetry, Spanish –
History and criticism. | LCSH: Spanish poetry – To 1500 –
History and criticism.
Classification: LCC PQ6381.B35 2023 | DDC 861/.109–dc23

Cover design: Val Cooke
Cover image: Rodrigo offering the head of Ximena's father to his own father
as confirmation that the latter's humiliation has been avenged. Illustration by
René Ben Sussan from Robert Southey's *Chronicle of the Cid*.

Support for the publication of this book was provided by the
Class of 1956 Provost's Faculty Development Endowment at
Washington and Lee University.

We wish to acknowledge the land on which the University of
Toronto Press operates. This land is the traditional territory of the
Wendat, the Anishnaabeg, the Haudenosaunee, the Métis, and the
Mississaugas of the Credit First Nation.

University of Toronto Press acknowledges the financial support of
the Government of Canada, the Canada Council for the Arts, and
the Ontario Arts Council, an agency of the Government of Ontario,
for its publishing activities.

Contents

Acknowledgments

The *Mocedades de Rodrigo* was the focus of my MA thesis and has been a recurring subject of interest ever since. The journey to the completion of this book has involved numerous stages and varying degrees of urgency and interest. The participation of prominent senior scholars and like-minded colleagues in the publication of the collection of essays I organized on the *Mocedades* (1999) was a timely reminder of the long-standing critical interest in the work and of the promise for new avenues of inquiry. The encouragement, guidance, and ultimately collaboration of Prof. David Hook in that process was instrumental in bringing the project to its successful conclusion. The fact that he and more senior colleagues entrusted their work to a relative newcomer was instrumental to the success of the project and set a high standard for subsequent collaborations.

A few years later, a trusted colleague suggested that I make publication inquiries regarding a bilingual edition of the *Mocedades* text that I had prepared as a companion to my online edition of the *Cantar de mio Cid*. Richard K. Emmerson, at the time executive director of the Medieval Academy of America, was very encouraging in his response to my proposal and helped shepherd the book towards publication in the Medieval Academy Book Series of the University of Toronto Press, under the direction of the Humanities acquisitions editor Suzanne Rancourt (2007). The relative success of that edition was especially heartening and critical in overcoming the general perception that the narrative of the deeds of the young Cid was a secondary text, a kind of literary outlier and for that reason unworthy of the same critical attention as the masterful narrative of the mature Cid.

A more recent stimulus for the completion of this book was the inauguration of a series of volumes on Charlemagne as a European icon, directed by Prof. Marianne Ailes of the University of Bristol, under the auspices of the Société Rencesvals, for which I organized a volume on the literary and historiographical legacy of Charlemagne in Spain (2016). The Charlemagne project was prominently funded by the Leverhulme Trust and included invited talks, conference sessions, planning meetings, seminars, and a month-long stay at the University of Bristol highlighted by fruitful academic exchanges with faculty and graduate students. Subsequent to the publication of the Spain volume, participants presented their findings in a panel at a well-attended conference session in Kalamazoo, Michigan. My contribution was a new reading of the final episode of the *Mocedades*, the Spanish invasion of France, in which I traced its origins to earlier legendary responses to Charlemagne's incursion into Spain. This trajectory in turn supported some of the overarching findings of this book, that the Rodrigo narrative is not a latter-day epic poem, or a prequel to the narrative of the mature Cid; it is rather an epic narrative steeped in a long tradition of heroic tales that date from the earliest recorded nativist writings on Charlemagne's Spanish campaign.

The analysis of the early modern portrayal of Rodrigo and Ximena in Guillén de Castro's play *Mocedades del Cid* benefitted from a lively exchange with colleagues and undergraduate students at Colby College in the fall of 2017. Their queries and a subsequent anonymous review led to a fuller integration of the second part of Guillén's drama *Las mocedades del Cid-Comedia segunda*, as well as Pierre Corneille's *Le Cid*, into what is now the final chapter of this book. The chapter on Rodrigo's celestial companions benefitted from the discussion emanating from the audience at a regional conference (SEMA Conference 2017). That event and its participants were instrumental in furthering inquiries into the role of Saint Lazarus in Rodrigo's pilgrimage to the shrine of Saint James at Compostela.

The remaining chapters represent efforts to clarify some of the more vexing and stimulating questions related to the Rodrigo narrative, such as the chronicle narration and its relationship to the epic, and the latter's narrative coherence. Conference presentations and their attendant audiences all figure prominently herein as well, and I wish to thank them as well, albeit anonymously.

All of this is meant to describe a long trajectory in the gestation and final realization of this book. Apart from the milestones identified above, all of us who have laboured to better understand the Rodrigo narrative also owe a significant debt of gratitude to the pioneers of the field. Their inquiries into the narrative's origins, its place in the epic canon, its manifestation in the ballad tradition, and the nature and the provenance of the unique manuscript of the poem animated their collective accomplishments and have served as a touchstone for those of us who followed. Among these accomplished scholars, I was very fortunate to have studied with Thomas Montgomery, to have enjoyed the generous camaraderie of Samuel Armistead, and to have benefitted from the support and example of Alan Deyermond. Additionally, the significant advances made by my contemporaries Leonardo Funes, Alberto Montaner, and Mercedes Vaquero have shaped the findings in these pages much more than the occasional references to their work might indicate.

Washington and Lee University, where this project started and now concludes, has been a steady source of support, through yearly Lenfest research grants, two sabbatical leaves, and the encouragement of three deans and two provosts. My family, of course, two daughters who have been ever curious and open-minded, inquiring and encouraging as I laboured on, and my wife and partner, with projects of her own but always willing to listen and advise, and who from the very earliest stage of this project saw its potential. To all of you, my sincerest gratitude.

SPEAKING TRUTH TO POWER

Introduction

The narrative of the deeds of the young Rodrigo, before he became Cid, first emerges in the initial chapters of the *Crónica de Castilla* (c. 1300), interspersed among the deeds of King Fernando I of León and Castile. The potent vibrancy of the legendary deeds of this young Castilian warrior contrasts notably with the uninspired, matter-of-fact narrative of the reign of Fernando I that was taken verbatim from the *Estoria de España* (1284). The narrative of Rodrigo's youth is also the subject of an epic poem, the *Mocedades de Rodrigo*. Although the characterization of king and vassal contrasts dramatically in the two texts, chronicle and epic recreate essentially the same story. An additional important factor linking the two narrations is that the unique poetic text and the prose chronicle have been preserved in the same manuscript, written in the same copyist hand. The manuscript has been dated to as late as 1400, but the youthful deeds of the young Cid that are manifested in the poem surely originated with an oral narrative that predates its incorporation into the recycled chronicle narration of the deeds of King Fernando.

Scholars have variously claimed that one or the other of these two narratives is more authentic, as in closer to an oral or a non-extant pre-existing written version, based on the divergent portrayals of the main protagonists and of their relationship in chronicle and poem. In the chronicle text, Rodrigo is a respectful and loyal vassal of the king, who in turn is mature and decisive in his endeavours and in encouraging Rodrigo's allegiance through the abundant gifts and praise that he bestows on his prize vassal. In the poem, Fernando is young, indecisive, and ineffectual as a ruler and consequently cannot count on the support of the grandees of his kingdom, most pointedly the Castilians. The most noteworthy difference in the two narrations is the characterization of Rodrigo, whom scholars often refer to as rebellious, but might be better appreciated as a self-assured, independent-minded, clear-thinking, and fearsome warrior. His most salient characteristic is his willingness to take up arms to fight for what he believes is right. He first battle is to defend his family against the aggression of another prominent family. He then engages in a series of combats in an effort to maintain his own independence and self-determination. Subsequently he leads the battle against traitorous Castilian counts who plotted to kill their king. Later, after his personal circumstances have changed dramatically, he aligns himself with King Fernando in the defence of the sovereignty of Spain against foreign aggressors.

The final battles of Rodrigo's youth against a union of European powers led by the King of France reflect a long tradition in Spanish legendary literature that emerges in response to the historical invasion of Spain by Charlemagne in 778. Spanish medieval chronicles, first in Latin and later written in the vernacular, document attitudes and anonymous acts of heroic defiance against the invading Franks until there emerges a legendary warrior from Asturias who defies his acquiescent king and gathers an army to repel the foreign invaders. This fearless warrior, Bernardo del Carpio, in his repulsion of the Frankish invaders of Spain, provides the mould from which the legendary Rodrigo is cast. They are both fiercely independent and respond defiantly to the demand for tribute or the threat of invasion, while those around them are helpless to act or counsel appeasement.

The exploration of the parallels between these two narratives provides further insights into the resemblance to another warrior who took the initiative in defence of his country against the invading Franks, this time from the perspective of a twelfth-century French *chanson de geste*, *Fierabras*. The eponymous Spanish Muslim protagonist of this poem is portrayed in a solitary defiant stand against the Twelve Peers of France and their king to meet him in combat at the gates of Paris, a challenge also made by Rodrigo in a setting and with phrasing almost identical to that of Fierabras. These parallels between Rodrigo and Bernardo, and then again between Rodrigo and Fierabras, compel us to question the assumptions behind efforts to establish a fixed date for the creation of this legendary tale that emerges intermittently through prose chronicles before its attachment to the young Cid in epic poem and prose chronicle. The tale clearly had a dynamic existence in oral diffusion across centuries of creative storytelling. In the face of this mingling of narratives, languages, cultures, religions, and historical facts and legends, the questions of precedence and authenticity seem, to put it kindly, somewhat beside the point.

In previous studies the divergent portrayals of Rodrigo in chronicle and poem have been analysed mostly as a means of establishing precedence of one composition over the other. The chronicle is learned and courtly in nature, and it follows that Rodrigo's characterization as an obedient and deferential vassal to a mature and respected King Fernando should reflect its compositional milieu and purpose. It is well aligned with an effort on the part of the royal court and the learned clerics in its employ to bolster the image of the monarchy in the initial period of the minority of King Fernando IV (born 1285, ruled 1295–1312). The portrayal of Rodrigo in the poem as defiantly independent and unwilling to commit himself in vassalage to a young, inexperienced, and insecure Fernando I, represents a different perspective on what is surely the same circumstance: A young king who is indecisive and incapable of imposing his will upon his enemies and unruly vassals without the support of a wilful and domineering Castilian warrior. These two versions may well have been competing for prominence at the same time, perhaps tailored to different audience expectations, or the poem may have served as an edifying tale of caution during the minority of the orphaned son of Fernando IV, Alfonso XI (born 1311, ruled 1312–50).

Although these two textual manifestations of the Rodrigo narrative are important, and it would be instructive to know which of them appeared first, this study adopts a wider focus and takes a longer view. It begins with the assumption that behind each textual manifestation of this heroic narrative lies an active oral narrative tradition, virtually imperceptible to modern readers. By tracing this vibrant heroic narrative as it emerges from the oral tradition that sustains it onto parchment text, from its earliest manifestation in the aftermath of Charlemagne's disastrous retreat from his imperial mission in Spain to the early modern drama of Guillén de Castro, we can identify the permutations that propelled its continuing popularity. In some instances these changes may be attributable to individual authors who laboured to adapt the inherited material to new audience expectations or to the exigencies of a particular literary genre. Likewise, this methodology will enable us to recognize the heroic qualities of the protagonist and whether they have persisted over time or adapted to new expectations. In any case, every version of this heroic narrative will have reconciled the tradition from which it drew its inspiration with the aesthetic principles of author and audience and their expectations for heroic conduct.

A case in point is the episode of Rodrigo's knighting ceremony. The chronicle text relates the knighting of Rodrigo after the historical siege and conquest of Coimbra by Fernando I, an episode that is not narrated in the poem. Yet important components of the Coimbra episode – King Fernando's pilgrimage to Santiago to seek divine assistance for his siege and Rodrigo's knighting – are narrated in the epic text as parts of other episodes. Fernando I's conquest of Coimbra is historical fact, but Rodrigo's knighting ceremony is boisterous fiction, appended to the episode in order to accommodate the growth of his legendary status. In the poem, Rodrigo's knighting takes place in the heat of the struggle against the army of France, as part of an entirely legendary episode. What seems most impressive about the narration of these events is the artistry with which they were incorporated into their respective contexts, drawing no attention to themselves, serving to move the narration forward in the same fashion as what came before and what followed. As indicators of authenticity, or of the originality of one version of the story over the other, the narration of these events can tell us very little, but as indicators of the ability of writers and the purveyors of oral narrative to incorporate new material into an ongoing narrative tradition, they are highly instructive.

In addition to the tracing of the trajectory of the Rodrigo narrative and its permutations through time, this study also addresses the critical issue that has garnered by far the most attention among scholars of the Spanish epic, the quest for narrative coherence in the *Mocedades*. Early readings of the poem understood it as the poorly preserved narration of a rite of passage for the young protagonist, a ritualized coming-of-age story in which Rodrigo vowed to delay his marriage and service to the king until he had won five battlefield victories. Subsequent studies supported this interpretation of the poem by identifying thematic parallels between Rodrigo's first combat and his subsequent return to civil society and the Irish epic saga *Táin Bó Cúailnge* and the initiation rite of its hero, Cú Chulainn. A poorly copied manuscript, an inattentive copyist, and a later prosaic clerical hand have all contributed to the difficulty in reaching a consensus on just which battles should be counted among the five that Rodrigo vowed to win, or whether his vow was fulfilled before the final battle of the poem, Spain's invasion of France. Other ways of understanding progression in the poem have also been advanced, such as the gradual flowering of the alliance between Rodrigo and King Fernando, or the melding of the public and the private spheres in a triumphal allegiance that benefits king and vassal. Finally, a few readings eschew the search for cohesion and posit that the poem is simply a series of episodes linked by a single protagonist, or that its author employed a compositional principle that privileges fragmentation and heterogeneous actors.

The analysis formulated herein points to a unifying theme in the poem, that of a strong-willed and therefore exemplary protagonist throughout, and identifies a progression in which Rodrigo sets the rules that at first estrange him from others, most notably his king, but that eventually lead to absolute trust in his counsel and a belated recognition of his ability to forge highly beneficial alliances. This progression plays out through a series of affective encounters in which the deep humanity of the poem's protagonists is on full display. We see them in moments of high pathos, when they are literally beside themselves, and this vulnerability generates transcendent moments that lead to a deeper mutual understanding and create the psychic space that makes possible new and fruitful allegiances. Rodrigo's encounters with other protagonists, initially commandeered by Ximena, but later with King Fernando and other actors in the poem, reflect this understanding, although probably neither the narrator nor the audience would have been capable of articulating it. The narrative coherence of the poem can be found, counterintuitively, in isolated moments, when all action ceases and we are witness to the effect that Rodrigo has on others, initially of disbelief, but, as the poem progresses, the creation of lasting admiration and unyielding allegiance.

Scholarship on the *Mocedades* is vast and because some of the most prominent scholars of medieval Spanish literature have dedicated themselves to one or another of its intriguing features, it is nearly overwhelming in its reach and significance. It begins with the pioneering and lasting import of the early scholarship on classifying the poem, reaching a consensus on its physical presentation, followed by the studies on its meaning and its relationship to other narratives of the Spanish epic and especially to the traditional understanding of its protagonist, the younger version of the mature Cid. This critical foundation allowed a subsequent generation of scholars to open new avenues of inquiry and to begin to see influence on the poem from other narrative traditions. A more recent generation of scholarship on the poem has assimilated these findings and moved into a period of reflection, of fine-tuning previous findings and making broader sense of a confounding textual and legendary enigma.

The present contribution to an enhanced appreciation of the narrative of Rodrigo's youth has incorporated a good deal of the vast scholarship that has gone before, reviewed it, and blended it into the context of new critical perspectives on some of its most studied aspects, the narrative traditions that are reflected in it, and its revival in early modern Spanish literature. Readers should gain a heightened appreciation for the vibrancy of the poetic tradition that lives beyond the texts we study, the oral narratives that are continually refashioned for new audiences and contexts. But most of all, the Rodrigo that emerges from the pages of this study is not the reckless, arrogant, or raging warrior that we may have reckoned. From his earlier emergence in prose chronicles through the vernacular narratives, ballads, and early modern dramas, Rodrigo is more exemplary than rebellious, a paragon of right-thinking, bravery, decisiveness, Christian charity, and a willingness to speak truth to power and to fight for freedom against those who would subjugate him, his family, the Castilian nation or Spain. His leadership qualities first emerge in his role as a *parrhesiastes*, both in the sense of saying what is true and in speaking truth to power. This is the essence of his magnetism, and as he evolves into the leader that his king and country need, and through his exemplarity in words and deeds, Rodrigo inspires others. The chapters that follow will reveal these characteristics hiding in plain sight, and through their examination the rich complexity of this narrative figure will become manifest, offering insights for a better understanding of the narrative tradition from which he emerges and leading to a fulsome recalibration of the heroic qualities of the protagonists of the Spanish epic.

Chapter One

The Legendary Response to Charlemagne in Spain

This chapter begins by examining the role of Charlemagne's invasion of Spain as the catalyst for the development of a versatile and imaginative epic narrative tradition of heroic responses by legendary Spanish warriors.[1] This process crystalized in narratives celebrating the legendary deeds of Bernardo del Carpio, and after several permutations culminated in the final episode of the *Mocedades de Rodrigo,* or the youthful deeds of Rodrigo. These narratives counter the perception derived from a long history of critical readings of the *Cantar de Mio Cid (Cantar),* that the Spanish epic recreates the lives of historical figures and that its portrayal of them and of the events in which they participate has its basis in historical events.[2] The creative response to the Frankish invasion did not exist outside of history, of course. Charlemagne did indeed invade Spain, and his campaign is recorded in Spanish sources nearly contemporary with the emerging literary response, but the lifeblood of the narratives of Bernardo and Rodrigo lies in the French *Chansons de geste,* not in the historical invasion. This chapter begins with a brief historical review of Charlemagne's campaign in Spain, its portrayal in Carolingian chronicles and the initial response in Spanish sources. Its focus then moves to an early legendary version of the historical event, followed by the emergence of the fictional Asturian warrior Bernardo del Carpio, who rises to the defence of his homeland against the invading Franks. The subsequent transformations and innovations of the evolving Bernardo narrative culminate with the portrayal of the young Cid as the leader of the defence of Spain against the threat of invasion by the king of France. It concludes with the description of the heroic stand of Rodrigo as he challenges the Twelve Peers of France at the gates of Paris.

Prior to undertaking an analysis of narratives centred on Charlemagne's invasion of Spain in 778, a review of that historical event is in order. Its purpose here is to allow us to mark the distance between the historical event and its treatment in later epic narrative, the focus of this study. Sulayman ibn al-A'rabi, the pro-Abbasid *amir* of Barcelona and Girona, along with his co-conspirators al-Husayn ibn Sa'd ibn Ubada, *wali* of Zaragoza, and the unidentified *wali* of Huesca, travelled to Charlemagne's Diet of Paderborn in Westphalia in the spring of 777. They were concerned that the Umayyad *amir* of al-Andalus, 'Abd al-Rahman I, had grown so powerful that all regional autonomy, Muslim and Christian, was endangered. They proposed a military alliance in which Sulayman and al-Husayn promised to secure the approaches for an invasion and occupation of northern Hispania by Frankish armies, in return for protection from a consolidating Córdoba. The three pro-Abbasid rulers also conveyed that the almighty Abbasid caliph at Baghdad, Muhammad al-Mahdi, was also concerned about the Umayyad prince's centralizing designs and had promised an invasion force. When the army of the Franks arrived in Pamplona, the great walled city opened their gates to them, but at Zaragoza, al-Husayn refused entrance to the Franks and their allies. The ensuing siege had lasted just a month when the news of a Saxon rebellion and depredations reaching well west of the Rhine precipitated Charlemagne's retreat. To make matters worse, the wary Basques of Pamplona had shut the gates of their city to the retreating Franks, denying them the possibility of using it as a base for winter quarters. Charlemagne turned his wrath on the Christian city and destroyed it and its walls, severely chastising its inhabitants. This act of malice roused the Basques to revenge, leading to the slaughter of Charlemagne's rearguard (historical synopsis is based on Lewis 244–53).

The first contemporaneous account we have of Charlemagne's campaign in Spain is found in the *Royal Frankish Annals* (*Annales regni Francorum*), a history of the Carolingian dynasty that begins with the death of Charles Martel (741 CE), records the major events of the reign of Charlemagne, and ends with the entry for the year 829, midway through the reign of Louis the Pious (814–40 CE). The entries for 793 onward are contemporaneous with the events they describe (Scholz and Rogers 5). Although in the original entry for the year 778 the Battle of Roncesvalles is not recounted, there is the mention of a pre-invasion visit to the general assembly convened at Paderborn in 777, in which "Saracens from Spain also came to the assembly, ibn al-Arabi and his son Deiuzefi – in Latin, Joseph – as well as his son-in-law" (*Royal Frankish Annals* 55–6). For the year 778, the author of the *Annals* describes Charlemagne's incursion into Spain and arrival at Zaragoza, and then continues: "The king received hostages from ibn al-Arabi and Abu Taher and many Saracens, destroyed Pamplona, and subjugated the Spanish Basques and the people of Navarre. Then he returned to Francia" (56).[3]

Although in the original account there is no mention of the Battle of Roncesvalles for the year 778, a later revision to the entry inserts a description of the battle as taking place "on the heights of the Pyrenees," of the ambush by the Basques, their attack on the rearguard, the killing of the unnamed "officers of the palace," the plundering of the baggage, and the vanishing of the enemy, all of which "shadowed the king's view of his success in Spain" (*Royal Frankish Annals* 56). The names of the Frankish princes who died in the battle are not given, and no connection is made between the destruction of Pamplona by Charlemagne and the subsequent slaughter of the Frankish rearguard in ambush by the Basques.

More detail and personal perspective characterize the description of Charlemagne's Spanish campaign in Einhard's *Vita Karoli Magni* (c. 830). This text is considered the most valued historical source for the reign of Charlemagne, in part because the author was his trusted friend and therefore able to "base much of his biography of the emperor on personal experience" (Scherabon Firchow and Zeydel 13). The chapter on the Spanish campaign (chapter 9) is brief, like the others in the book, equivalent to a typed page in length. Einhard describes how in the course of the war against the Saxons, Charlemagne decided to invade Spain "Hispaniam ... agreditur," but gives no reason for the aggression, or a specific date. He crossed the Pyrenees and accepted the surrender of all the towns and castles that he attacked "omnibus, quae adierat, oppidis atque castellis in deditionem acceptis." The biographer identifies none of the places conquered, nor is there any mention of their inhabitants, or whether they were Christian or Muslim. Charlemagne then crossed back over the mountains safe and sound "salvo et incolomi," except that he briefly happened to experience the perfidious Basques "praeter ... Wasconiam perfidiam parumper in redeundo contigit experiri" (Einhard 54). This brief encounter, as it turns out, is the massacre of Charlemagne's rearguard.

The author then describes the attack by the Basques, how they had laid in ambush at the summit of the mountain "in summi montis," attacking the end of the baggage "extremam impedimentorum partem" and those troops at the very rear who were marching in support of those ahead, whom they protected "et eos qui novissimi agminis incedentes subsidio praecedentes tuebantur." They forced them into the adjacent valley and, engaging them in battle, killed them all to the last man "in subiectam vallem deiciunt consertoque cum eis proelio usque ad unum onmes interficiunt." The author distinguishes Eggihard, overseer of the royal table, Anselm, palace count, and Roland, prefect of the frontier, from among the many who were killed "In quo proelio Eggihardus regiae mensae praepositus, Anshelmus comes palatii et Hruodlandus Britannici limitis praefectus cum aliis conpluribus interficiuntur." After seizing the baggage, the Basques scattered under cover of darkness "ac direptis impedimentis, noctis beneficio, quae iam instabat, protecti summa cum celeritate in diversa desperguntur." This circumstance helped the Basques, along with their light armor and the terrain, against the heavy armor of the Franks and the unevenness of the place "Adiuvabat in hoc facto Wascones et levitas armorum et loci ... e contra Francos, et armorum gravitas et loci iniquitas." The fact that the enemy dispersed so completely that they left not the slightest clue to their whereabouts, to the present day (a temporal reference by Einhard) has made it impossible to avenge this deed "Neque hoc factum ad praesens vindicari poterat, quia hostis re perpetrata ita dispersus est, ut ne fama quidem remaneret, ubinam gentium quaeri potuisset" (Einhard 54).

Einhard feels compelled to explain this crushing defeat in terms of the advantages exploited by the Basques, the terrain that suited their quick movement and their light armor. He also ascribes the absence of any retaliatory actions by Charlemagne to the onset of night and the virtual vanishing of the enemy, who left no trace to follow. Clearly the massacre of the rearguard of the Franks and the looting of their baggage train troubled the emperor's biographer more than might be implied by his initial offhand reference to a brief encounter with the perfidious Basques. These insights into the mindset of the emperor's biographer as he reprised the battle and its significance are a touchstone of sorts for the subsequent legendary life of the battle and will help us more fully appreciate some of the nuance of the later accounts of the encounter at Roncesvalles.[4]

A brief marginal gloss in a manuscript dated to the third quarter of the eleventh century constitutes the first textual record of an oral narrative on Charlemagne's Spanish campaign. Known as the *Nota Emilianense*, the gloss is named for the monastery where the manuscript was produced, San Millán (de la Cogolla), near Nájera, in the region of the *Rioja Alta*, in north-central Spain, just fourteen kilometres from the pilgrim route to Santiago de Compostela.[5] The text is brief, the equivalent of one modern-day paragraph. Although it might appear to summarize an early version of the *Chanson de Roland*, the text is unique in meaningful ways (Bennett 61–2). The names of the Frankish princes familiar to us from the *Roland* appear Hispanicized, as does the placename of the battle, *Rozaballes* (Alonso 64). These characteristics point to an oral narrative tradition that over time would have worked its way from France onto the pilgrimage route into Spain and eventually onto the *Nota* (Duggan 66–7).

The *Nota* correctly dates the arrival of Charlemagne at Zaragoza "In era dcccxui (Hispanic Era 816, Christian Era 778) uenit Carlus rex ad Cesaragusta" (Alonso 9), from the perspective of a writer located in Spain ("uenire"). Literary or mnemonic devices are apparent, such as Charlemagne's twelve nephews, each one with three thousand mounted warriors and each one of them in turn with their own foot soldiers "habuit duodecim neptis un*usquisque* habebat tria milia ęquitu*m* cum loricis suis." Each of the twelve nephews served Charlemagne for just one month of the year (twelve months), with his vassals "Et un*usq*uisqu*e* singulos menses serbiebat ad regem cum scolicis suis." Finally, the narration of Charlemagne's arrival in Zaragoza, the shared determination to accept a large tribute to stave off starvation and return home, the distinctive portrayal of a powerful Roland "rodlane belligerator fortis" singled out to command the rearguard of the army, and the killing of Roland as the army traversed the pass of Cisera "At ubi exercitum portum de Sicera transiret," are motifs also featured in the *Roland*. Saracens are responsible for the death of Roland, "In Rozaballes a gentibus sarrazenorum fuit Rodlane occiso," not Basques as in the Frankish accounts, and Roland alone is memorialized in death, which underlines his prominent legendary status. Taken together, these details confirm that the *Nota* preserves portions of a narrative that derives its inspiration from a legendary source independent of the histories of the Carolingian court, an emergent *Roland* that was familiar to audiences in Spain.

The Carolingian accounts of Charlemagne's invasion are the foundation of its re-creation by the author of the *Historia Silensis*, an anonymous Latin chronicle that traces the history of the kingdom of León and Castile from the Visigoths to the reign of Alfonso VI, likely composed between 1118 and 1126 (Martin).[6] The passage is a brief three-paragraph entry, but very interesting in the way that it combines a narration of the recorded historical events with the author's defiant rejection of some of the claims contained in other, undocumented sources. The author also places the Frankish invasion within a wider historical context, which lends it additional meaning. The relevant passage comes directly after the relation of the Muslim conquest of Spain in 711, here dated to 709 (747 Hispanic Era), and attributed to Hulit, the mighty king of the barbarians of all of Africa "fortissimus rex barbarorum tocius Africe," led initially by the dishonoured Count Julian and two dispossessed sons of the deceased King Witiza (*Historia Silensis* 147; chap. 11). As the narrative moves forward, the author emphasizes the precarious situation of the Goths, abandoned by God and by people from other lands, none of whom are known to have come to their aid "nemo exterarum gentium Ispaniam subleuase cognoscitur," most pointedly Charlemagne "Sed neque Carolus" (149: chap. 12). The chronicler then rejects as false the assertions made by the Franks that Charlemagne liberated any cities in Spain from the hands of the pagans "quem infra Pireneos montes quasdam ciuitates a manibus paganorum eripuisse Franci falso asserunt" (149–50), just prior to undertaking his narration of Charlemagne's incursion into Spain.[7]

As in the version of the *Annals*, Charlemagne's incursion into Spain is precipitated by an offer from Sulaiman ibn al-Arabi ("Hybinnaralaby") to place himself and the province of Zaragoza, which he had governed in the name of 'Abd al-Rahman I "quem Cesaraugustano regno Abderrahaman, magnus rex Maurorum, prefecerat" (*Historia Silensis* 150), under the dominion of Charlemagne.[8] With the expectation of vanquishing one or more Spanish cities, Charlemagne marched his army across the Pyrenees to a joyous reception from the citizens of Pamplona, who were confined from every direction by the fury of the Moors "Quem ubi Pampilonenses uident, magno cum gaudio suscipiunt. Erant enim undique maurorum rabie coangustiati" (150). But upon arrival at Zaragoza, in the way of the Franks, Charles was corrupted by gold "more Francorum auro corruptus," and having never lifted a finger "absque ullo sudore" for the cause of delivering from the barbarians the domain of the Holy Church, he returned to his people "ad propia reuertitur" (150). Clearly, bellicose Spain is not intimidated by toga-wearing invaders, but only by hardened warriors "Quippe bellatrix Ispania duro non togato milite concutitur" (150). In fact, Charles fervently desired to bathe in the hot baths that he had so lavishly constructed in Aachem "Anelabat etenim Carolus in thermis illis cicius lauari, quas Aquis Grani ad hoc opus deliciose construxerat" (150).[9]

The author then relates that on his return through the Pyrenees, Charlemagne endeavoured to destroy Pamplona, a Muslim city "Panpiloniam maurorum opidum destruere conaretur," and that the majority of his army paid a great price for their temerity: "magnas exsoluit penas" (150). Since the army was large and had to march through the narrow pass, it was obliged to stretch out. The rear of the army, protecting those farther ahead, was attacked by Navarrese descending from the heights above. Engaging with them in battle, the Navarrese killed them all to the last man "Siquidem cum agmine longo, ut angusti loci situs permitebat, porrectus iret exercitus, extremum agmen, quod precedentes tuebatur, Nauarri desuper incursantes agrediuntur. Consertoque cum eis prelio, usque ad unum omnes interficiunt" (150–1). The author then gives the names of the prominent Franks killed in the battle, identical to those in the *Vita*: "Eggihardus mense Caroli regis prepositus, Anselmus, sui palacii comes et Rotholandus Britanicus prefectus," along with the slaughter of many unnamed others "cum aliis conpluribus ceciderunt" (151). Also in accordance with the *Vita*, the author asserts that this deed remains unavenged to this day "Quod factum usque in hodiernum diem inultum permansit" (151). Although the *Historia Silensis* and the *Vita* identify the attackers differently (Wascones vs. Navarri), to a twelfth-century Leonese chronicler they were the same people, and the wording throughout is otherwise similar enough to confirm the *Vita* as an important source for the author of the *Silensis*.

The most salient elements of this passage are the defiant tone of the author toward the assertions of Frankish conquests made in Spain, the identification of the fierce warrior culture of Spain as an incentive for the return of the Franks to their homeland, and of course the emphasis on the unavenged slaughter of the rearguard of Charlemagne's army. The assertion that Pamplona was a Muslim city when Charlemagne endeavoured to destroy it is a puzzling inaccuracy, given the previous description of the city as receptive to Charlemagne and his invading army. This perceived misconception may be the result of the author trying to rationalize Charlemagne's attack on what he first identified as a Christian Pamplona. In any case, Pamplona was peopled by Basques, and the author seems to link its destruction to the subsequent retaliation by the Basques on the Frankish rearguard, who are portrayed in their defeat as paying for their sins "magnas exsoluit penas" (*Historia Silensis* 150). Overall, the author of the *Silensis* colours his narration of Charlemagne's exploits in Spain with a native defiance that was most likely felt by audiences across northern Spain as they listened to minstrels singing of the heroic exploits of the Franks in their homeland.[10]

It is not clear exactly when the poets and audiences of oral narratives like the one summarized in the *Nota* turned their attention away from the Franks to the warriors responsible for their slaughter. The author of the *Historia Silensis*, so defiant in his response to the Carolingian claims of conquests in Spain, would surely have embraced a more Hispanocentric version of the same events had once been known to him. In time, a warrior capable of defeating the Franks does emerge from the highlands of Asturias, the birthplace of the resistance against the Muslims and the ancestral homeland of the Leonese monarchy. When he first emerges in the pages of the *Chronicon mundi* (c. 1236), Bernardo del Carpio is a fully formed fictional character. The chronicle author, Lucas, later bishop of Tuy (Tudensis, a.k.a. el Tudense), identifies Bernardo as the nephew of King Alfonso II of Asturias. It seems safe to assume that this hero of the Spanish resistance was forged in a native tradition of epic narration that no longer identified with the heroes of the French epic memorialized in the *Nota*. He represents a Spanish audience with enough pride and sense of accomplishment to imagine one of its own repelling an invasion by an army of Franks.

The episode involving Charlemagne's incursion into Spain and the defeat of the rearguard of his army at Roncesvalles is contained in one chapter of the chronicle, constituting about 1.5 pages of text (Tudensis 235-6; book 4, chap. 15, lines 1–39). In this account, Charlemagne has driven the Muslims out of France and restored the Christian cult "usque ad montes Pireneos expulsis Sarracenis restituit cultui Christiano" (lines 4–5). He then traverses the mountains of Roncesvalles "transciectis etiam Roscideuallis montibus" (line 5) and subjects to his rule the Goths and Spaniards who were in Catalonia and in the mountains of the Basque region "in montibus Vasconie" and in Navarre (line 7). Charlemagne writes to Alfonso II of Asturias demanding that Alfonso recognize him as suzerain, an act that infuriates his nephew, Bernardo.[11] Filled with rage, Bernardo rushes with his men "cum suis" (line 9) to join forces with Marsil, the Muslim king of Zaragoza, against Charlemagne. Charlemagne lays siege to Tudela, which he later abandons due to the treachery of Ganalon, but then conquers Nájera and Monte Jardín "montem Iardinum" (line 13) before initiating his return to France. Marsil, the Muslim king of Zaragoza, gathers his army and, together with Bernardo and some Navarrese allies "Bernaldo atque quibusdam Nauarris secum asociatis" (lines 15–16), attacks the Franks as they are retreating from Spain. As in the *Roland*, Charlemagne had already traversed the pass at Roncesvalles when the Muslims, here led by Bernardo, attack the rearguard of the French army:

> Et cum Francis inito bello Rodlandus, Britannicus prefectus, Anselmus comes, Egiardus, mense Caroli prepositus, cum aliis multis nobilibus Francis exigentibus peccatis nostrorum occisi sunt. Transierat iam quidem Carolus in primo suorum agmine Alpes Rocideuallis dimissa in posteriore parte exercitus manu robustorum ob custodiam, qui, Bernaldo, postposito Dei timore, super eos cum Sarracenis accerrime incursante, interfecti sunt.
>
> (lines 16–23)

> And having initiated the battle with the Franks, Roland, prefect of Brittany, Count Anselm, Eggihard, overseer of Charles's table, along with many other Frankish nobles were killed, in payment for (requiring it) our sins. Charles had already traversed the Roncesvalles Alps with the first of

his troops and left the rearguard of his army in the care of the strongest men. These were killed by Bernardo, who had set aside his fear of God and attacked them violently with the Saracens.[12]

Unlike the previous sources examined above, Charlemagne regroups his army and avenges the massacre of his knights by killing innumerable Muslim nobles "uiriliter uindicauit ex Sarracenorum nobilibus innumerabilem extinguens multitudinem" (lines 24–5). Additional events are recounted, but not in anything resembling a coherent narrative. Charlemagne pays homage to Saint James the Apostle by visiting his shrine in Santiago, trekking off the beaten path through Álava "per deuia Alaue veniens" (line 26). Then, returning to his Frankish kingdom "Germania," Charlemagne took Bernardo with him in great honour "Carolus autem reuertens in Germaniam secum cum honore magno Bernaldum detulit" (lines 34–5), and he slept in the Lord in Aachen, reaching the end of his life blissfully, where he rests in deserved honour.[13]

The retaliatory attack by Charlemagne is familiar to us from the *Roland*, but the narration by Lucas is noteworthy in certain other details. Charlemagne reverses course and wreaks vengeance on the Muslims who attacked his baggage train and killed his rearguard. Although Marsil and Bernardo had led a combined force of Christians and Muslims, in the counterattack the Franks kill only Muslims, with no mention of Bernardo, his vassals, or the Navarrese warriors allied with him. Lucas seems to truly delight in recounting the slaughter described in the counterattack, but it is a Christian victory over Muslims, or as Lucas formulates it: a most Christian Charles who avenged this deed in a triumphal victory over an innumerable multitude of Muslim nobles "Sed iterum Christianissimus Carolus exercitu reparato hoc factum triumphali uictoria uiriliter uindicauit ex Sarracenorum nobilibus innumerabilem extinguens multitudinem" (lines 23–5). Also, if we look again at the description of the initial battle, it no longer seems clear which side Lucas supports. In his narration, Lucas struggles with the image of Christians fighting each other. The principals of the Frankish rearguard were killed paying for our sins "exigentibus peccatis nostrorum" ["requiring it our sins"] (lines 18–19), while Bernardo killed the Frankish nobles by laying aside his fear of God "postposito Dei timore" (lines 21–2). In this account, the avenging counterattack seems to restore order, although Bernardo and his army are no longer present in the narration.

Since the *Vita* and the *Silensis* expressly deny any counterattack by Charlemagne, and the *Annals* and the *Nota* make no mention of one, it is possible that the Bernardo narrative never included a retaliatory attack.

The *Roland*, on the other hand, features an elaborate counterattack against the Muslim forces responsible for the slaughter of the Frankish rearguard, perhaps as early as 1100, but certainly by the time of the writing of the *Pseudo Turpin* (c. 1140), which includes an idiosyncratic version of the episode.[14] Thus, the counterattack described by Lucas would likely belong to the narrative tradition of the *Roland*, while the story of Bernardo and King Marsil joining forces and prevailing against the Franks represents a Spanish narrative tradition whose heroes would not have been slaughtered by the avenging Franks. Lucas's ambivalence towards Bernardo and his killing of the Franks may have moved him to conclude his narration of the episode with the annihilation of the Muslim nobles, retrieved from another source more to his liking.

The dynamic nature of the narrative tradition surrounding Bernardo del Carpio is emphatically affirmed when Lucas relates a second battle involving Bernardo, who this time joins forces with King Muza of Zaragoza (Tudensis 246–7; book 4, chap. 21, lines 1–22). The battle takes place in a valley of the Pyrenees "ad Clausuras Pireneorum moncium" (lines 4–5). The army of the Franks is routed, and many Romans and Gauls die in that massacre by the swords of Christians and Muslims "mox in fugam uersus est, et multi tam ex Romanis quam ex Gallis in illo excidio Christianorum et Sarracenorum gladiis perierunt" (lines 6–8). There is no retaliatory attack after this victory. In fact, Charles and King Alfonso become allies "Carolus postea cum rege Adefonso amiciciam fecit" (lines 8–9), and together they establish religious institutions and gain metropolitan status for Santiago. After which Charles returned to Francia peacefully "et pacifice in Franciam reuersus est" (line 13), taking with him his men who had been captured in battle by Alfonso, along with many other gifts generously conferred upon him "et alia multa dona illi largissime conferente" (line 15). Bernardo returned to his homeland with infinite spoils "cum infinita multitudine spoliorum in patriam se receipt" (lines 16–17). Lucas then reminds the reader that there were three Roman emperors named Charles: Charlemagne "Carolus Magnus," from the time of Alfonso the Chaste, under Pope Leo; Charles under Pope John; and this third one, Charles Martel. Lucas tries to distinguish between the two battles across time, but his sequence is wrong, and such specificity would hardly have been a concern to the audiences who surely relished hearing of the battlefield victories of Bernardo del Carpio and his Spanish Muslim allies against Charles, king of the Franks.

A subsequent and substantially different account of Charlemagne's invasion of Spain constitutes a single chapter in Rodrigo Jiménez de Rada's *Historia de rebus Hispanie* (c. 1242; pp. 126–8; book 4, chap. 10, lines 1–71). Jiménez de Rada was archbishop of Toledo (thus, El Toledano) when he wrote *De rebus* and is thought to have based his work on Lucas's *Chronicon*, reportedly with the intention of refuting it (Linehan 33). Yet, in this case at least, the archbishop's narration of Charlemagne's invasion of Spain is more than a refutation, it provides another version of the episode altogether. The most prominent innovations in El Toledano's narration are King Alfonso's voluntary submission of his kingdom to Charlemagne, the subsequent threat of rebellion by the lords of his court, the leadership of Alfonso in organizing a defensive force, the frontal strike by King Alfonso and Bernardo against the vanguard of the invading army of the Franks, and the absence of any Muslim involvement in the battle. In reviewing the episode, it should become clear that the archbishop supports his refutation of elements of Lucas's version with an alternate narrative, which he skillfully privileges over competing accounts.[15]

In El Toledano's narration, King Alfonso II of Asturias, who never married and had no heirs, is depicted as having tired of fighting the Muslim enemy. He sent ambassadors in secret to the king of the Franks, anachronistically styled emperor "ad imperatorem Carolum" (lines 3–4), and offered to leave his kingdom to Charlemagne in exchange for help against the unceasing Muslim menace "si ueniret in adiutorium" (line 6).[16] Charlemagne was himself engaged in warfare against Muslims in his own country and in the northeast of Spain, but agreed to the terms offered by the Asturian monarch. When the magnates of Alfonso's court learned of the agreement with Charlemagne, they threatened to expel Alfonso from the kingdom "ipsum a regno expellerent" and to secure for themselves another king "sibi de alio domino prouiderent" (lines 16–18). Above all the nobles present, Bernardo stood out in the degree of his vehemence in protest "in hiis instante forcius ceteris Berinaldo" (lines 19–20). Alfonso was understandably shaken by the threats "Rex … licet turbatus minis" (lines 20–1) and agreed to renege on his promise to Charlemagne. The emperor, enraged at Alfonso's change of heart, abandoned his campaign against the Muslims and attacked the Christian survivors of the Muslim raids in the mountains of Spain "direxit acies in reliquias Hispanorum" (line 24). This outrage against fellow Christians emboldened warriors from Asturias, Álava, Vizcaya, Navarre, Ruconia, and Aragón to rise up and join forces with Alfonso against the army of the Franks.

In the archbishop's description of the ensuing battle, Roland and his fellow nobles, Anselm and Eggihard, came in the vanguard of Charlemagne's army into Spain "In prima acie uenerunt Rollandus prefectus Britannie et Anselmus comes et Egiardus qui erat prepositus mense

Caroli" (lines 40–2). King Alfonso and his army charged them and by the power of their swords, vanquished them. Charlemagne, who was in the rear, sensed the destruction ahead of him and sounded the horn he was carrying, calling his men to retreat and regroup. The remaining vanguard rushed back to Charlemagne, in part because they were expecting Bernardo and an army of Muslims to attack the rearguard, but Bernardo stayed in the front with Alfonso, annihilating the vanguard of the Frankish army:

> Ad eum semianimes audita buccina confugerunt et ad eos qui extrema exercitus obseruabant propter Berinaldum, de quo fama erat quod cum exercitu Arabum per partes Aspe et Seole ueniebat postrema exercitus inuasurus; ipse tamen in strage primorum semper astitit Aldefonso.
>
> (lines 49–54)

> To him they fled half-dead, having heard the horn, and to those who guarded the rear of the army on account of Bernardo, of whom it was rumored that with an Arab army he was coming by way of Aspe and Soule to attack the rear of the army, yet he was always with Alfonso slaughtering the vanguard.

The only mention of Bernardo in the battle description is in the above citation, in which the rumors of a pending attack by Bernardo and an army of Arabs on the Frankish rearguard are acknowledged but ultimately denied. For Archbishop Rodrigo, King Alfonso led his army against the Franks, not Bernardo. They attacked the vanguard of the Frankish army, not the rearguard. Fellow Christians from all parts of northern Spain rose up to join Alfonso in the fight against Frankish aggression, not Muslims. And finally, Charlemagne, undone by the indignation and chaos surrounding him, returned to Germany to regroup, and to test Spain another day "Carolus, autem indignatione et confusione deiectus … ad Germaniam repedauit, ut reparato exercitu Hispaniam retemptaret" (lines 54–7). But the emperor lost himself in the delights of the hot springs of Aachen and died without ever avenging the defeat delivered at the hands of Alfonso. In fact, his magnificent tomb was inscribed with epitaphs of his early glories, while the space reserved for the threatened vengeance of (his defeat in) the Valles Caroli, became inglorious as he died unavenged "ea parte uacua remanente qua Valle Caroli uindictam minitans inglorius rediit et inultus" (lines 60–1).

The archbishop dedicates the remainder of the chapter to a legend that he identifies as propagated by jongleurs "Non nulli histrionum fabulis inherentes ferunt Carolum" (lines 61–2), that Charlemagne conquered many cities, castles, and fortresses across northern Spain and established the pilgrim route to Santiago from Germany and Gaul. These feats as reported by Jiménez de Rada correspond to yet another narrative of Charlemagne's incursions into Spain found in chapters 23–4 of the *Pseudo Turpin*. Although the archbishop acknowledges these claims by repeating them in detail, he ultimately rejects them in the subsequent chapter. He clarifies that these conquests attributed to Charlemagne are not credible since the facts demonstrate that the same cities were conquered within the last two hundred years (of his lifetime), and Charlemagne died more than four hundred years earlier (p. 130; book 4, chap. 11, lines 43–6).[17] This leads to his concluding thoughts on Charlemagne's incursion into Spain, that:

> Siue enim a Christianis, siue a Sarracenis ipse uel eius exercitus fuit uictus, itinere retrogrado comitatus dampnis et periculis retrocessit, nec stratum Sancti Iacobi suo itinere potuit publicare, cui non obuenit transitum Vallis Rocide penetrare. (lines 48–52)

> Whether by Christians or by Saracens, he or his army was vanquished, he returned from whence he came with ruin and suffering for company, nor could he open the route of Saint James [Santiago] on his march, he who did not manage to get through Roncesvalles.

In sum, we should note that the main thrust of Archbishop Rodrigo's narration refutes what Lucas had accepted as facts regarding Charlemagne's invasion of Spain. These include the rejection of any role for Muslims in the defence of Spain, the claim that King Alfonso attacked the vanguard of the Franks, the dispelling of the rumour of an attack on the Franks' rearguard by Muslims and Bernardo, and the absence of a devastating counterattack by Charlemagne. Also rejected is the assertion that Charlemagne conquered cities in Spain, or that he ever entered Spain, since he never managed to get through the pass at Roncesvalles "cui non obuenit transitum Vallis Rocide penetrare" (lines 51–2). In refuting the claims of Charlemagne's feats in Spain, the archbishop points with pride to his own ability to distinguish fact from fiction in the evaluation of sources "Facti igitur euidencie est pocius annuendum quam fabulosis narrationibus atendendum" (lines 46–7). It is interesting to note that the claims the archbishop most emphatically refutes, the conquest of cities in Spain, the attack on the rearguard, and the Muslim role in the defence of Spain, are today considered historically accurate, while the elements peculiar to his version, especially the voluntary submission of Alfonso to Charlemagne, Alfonso's attack on the Frankish vanguard in the company of Bernardo, and Charlemagne's inability to get through the Roncesvalles pass into Spain, seem to have no basis in fact.

It is worth noting here that the archbishop's denial of the leadership role that Lucas ascribed to Bernardo in the fight against the invading Franks and his privileging of King Alfonso are a precursor to the treatment of the young Cid in the *Crónica de Castilla* (c. 1300). In this account, the anonymous chronicler does not incorporate the independent spirit and aggressive leadership that characterize Rodrigo in the legendary material. He portrays the young Cid as an obedient vassal of King Fernando I, exemplary in other ways, but not as the contrarian voice of right-thinking before a hapless and insecure young king that we will see in the *Mocedades*.[18] Archbishop Rodrigo's proximity to royalty throughout his career seems to be a reasonable rationale for understanding his refashioning of the Bernardo legend as intentional, since his determination to emphasize the heroism and agency of King Alfonso in the defeat of Charlemagne can easily be linked to attitudes reflective of his position in society and within the Church. In these circles, leadership is the province of kings and the legendary feats of heroes like Rodrigo and Bernardo must cede their place of prominence in order to accommodate those beliefs.

At essentially the same time as Archbishop Rodrigo was completing his chronicle, the story of the defeat of Charlemagne by Bernardo del Carpio was being reformulated by a Castilian cleric, the anonymous author of the *Poema de Fernán González* (c. 1250).[19] The poem is a Castilian foundational narrative centred on the warrior deeds of its historical protagonist, Count Fernán González, a tenth-century magnate credited with winning for the county of Castile its independence from the kingdom of León. Prior to the emergence of the main protagonist in the narration, the poet reviews Spanish history from its conquest by the Goths, described as a great warrior people sent to Spain by Jesus Christ and subsequently inspired by the Holy Spirit to convert to Christianity. They became the light and guiding star of all Christendom, raising it up and crushing paganism, and, as the poet tells us, Count Fernán González did the same (vv. 23a–d). He and his subjects were an exceptional people, and as long as the world endures, they will never be forgotten: "e fueron de todo el mundo pueblo muy escogido,/ca en quanto el mundo durare nunca quedarán en olvido" (vv. 24b–c). After narrating the Muslim invasion of Spain and the heroic resistance by Pelayo of Asturias, the poet turns his attention to Charlemagne's Spanish campaign. In keeping with the poem's theme of Castilian exceptionalism,

Bernardo del Carpio and King Alfonso II are identified as Castilian, and their victory over Charlemagne is the inspiration for a litany of attributes that make Castile superior to all other lands: "Por esso vos digo aquesso, que bien lo entendades,/mejores son que otras tierras en las que vos morades" ["That's why I say this, that you should understand it well,/these lands in which you live are better than other lands"] (vv. 145a–b).

The Bernardo narrative in the *Fernán González* is unique in many ways, although clearly linked to the narratives examined thus far. As in the Lucas narrative, Bernardo fights twice against invading forces led by Charlemagne, here "el rey Carlos" ["King Charles"] (v. 127b). The march to the first battle begins with a missive from Charles to Alfonso that he intends to conquer Spain. Bernardo learns of the French plans and leads his own vassals and the army of King Alfonso to meet the French, who never advance past the Basque port of Fuenterrabia. According to a written source referenced by the poet, seven French kings and potentates died in this battle: "mató aí de Franceses reyes e potestades,/como dize la escritura siete fueron, que sepades" ["he killed there French kings and potentates/as the text says there were seven, know that"] (vv. 134a–b).[20] The French regroup and attack again, and this time Bernardo moves with his army to Zaragoza, to kiss the hand of King Marsil and to ask that his army of Castilians be permitted to lead the attack "against the Twelve Peers, those brave peoples" ["contra los doze pares, essos pueblos loçanos"] (v. 142d). The second battle takes place at the Aspe Pass, in the Central Pyrenees on the border between France and Spain. In neither of these battles as described in the *Fernán González* is there a retaliatory attack by Charlemagne, nor are the French kings and potentates who died in the first battle identified by name.[21]

It is noteworthy then that although the renowned warriors of the Franks are not mentioned in either narration of the two battles won by Bernardo, they are portrayed as exemplary in another episode of the poem, as part of a harangue by Fernán González meant to inspire his men to fight a Muslim army that is sure to annihilate them (vv. 343–51). In the harangue, the count reminds his men that both the dissolute "vicioso" and the suffering "lazrado" must die (v. 346a), and that only great deeds "buenos fechos" live on (v. 346c). Those who wished to accomplish great deeds endured extreme trials "por muy grandes trabajos ovieron a pasar" (v. 347b), they did not always have food to eat, and they had to forgo the pleasures of the flesh "los vicios de la carne anlos de olvidar" (v. 347d). Alexander's great deeds and battlefield victories are recalled, as is King David's killing of Goliath, and Judah

Maccabee, son of Matthias, and then the warriors from the *Chansons de geste*: "Carlos, Valdouinos, Roldán e don Ojero,/Terryn e Gualdabuey, e Vernald e Oliuero,/Torpyn e don Rivaldos e el gascón Angelero,/Estol e Salomon e el otro su conpanero" ["Charlemagne, Baudoin, Roland, Ogier le Danois, Thyerri l'Ardenois, Gandelbodus (rex Frisie), Arnaldus de Bellanda, Olivier, Torpyn, Renaud de Montauban, Engelenus (dux Aquitanie), Estol (comes Lingonensis), Salomon (socius Estulti)"] (vv. 352a–d).[22]

Fernán González deploys the names of these French warriors as models of self-sacrificing men worthy of emulation in a harangue meant to inspire his men to engage the outsized army of the Muslim foe. And, unlike in previous narratives, these warriors are not identified in the narration of the two heroic battlefield victories over Charlemagne. This seems to reinforce the notion mentioned earlier that the Bernardo narrative lives independently of the heroic depiction of the Franks in the *Roland*, each one having evolved through its own narrative tradition. In this formulation, a narrative of an attempted invasion of Spain by Charlemagne and his defeat by an army led by Bernardo del Carpio emerged over time. Bernardo and his Spanish army, either wholly Christian or a combined force of Christians and Muslims, are the heroes in this narrative tradition, not Charlemagne. Roland and his peers, along with their king, inhabit another narrative order in which they are as worthy of emulation as Alexander the Great, Judah Maccabee, and the young King David, eternal models of grandiose deeds, uncompromising faith, and courage in the face of impossible odds. These specific examples of heroism are a mixture of popular, sacred, and classical tales, very much in keeping with other formulations by the poet of the *Fernán González* (Bailey, *The Transformation*, 98–9).

The narrative of the deeds of Rodrigo, the young Cid, also features an episode that responds to the invasion threat posed by the king of France. In this episode Rodrigo has assumed the role of Bernardo, the guarantor of Castilian sovereignty. He takes his campaign to the very gates of Paris in the most elaborate and extravagant of the warrior deeds that constitute his march into manhood. Episodes from the narrative first appear in prose interspersed within the wider focus of the *Crónica de Castilla*, a textual reference that provides a secure date (c. 1300), a *terminus ante quem*, for the prominence of this narrative of Rodrigo's legendary youth (Gómez Redondo 138–41). The unique manuscript of the narrative in verse form, *Las mocedades de Rodrigo*,[23] relates essentially the same deeds celebrated in the chronicle, but in this rhymed version Rodrigo is portrayed as a twelve-year-old force of nature, primed for fight and at first openly hostile to Fernando I, king of Castile. The king is portrayed as an indecisive and ineffectual boy, and initially seems threatened by Rodrigo's aggressiveness and confidence. Their early encounters are fraught with tension, but when Rodrigo loses his father and uncles in battle, he makes the decision to support the king (*Las mocedades* v. 746). He subsequently assumes an active role in restoring order to the restive kingdom, becomes a trusted vassal, and as their relationship deepens, provides the young king with lessons in leadership. In the final episode of the poem, the king calls on Rodrigo to lead the armies of Spain in an invasion of France in retaliation for their demand for tribute.[24]

Parallels between the invasion episode in the *Mocedades de Rodrigo* (*MR*) and the Bernardo del Carpio narratives immediately come to mind, including the challenge to the sovereignty of a Spanish king delivered by letter or messenger, the lone angry reply by the hero, who then organizes an armed response, and the successful retaliation against the French enemy. Other details from the Bernardo narratives are absent, such as any engagement with the Muslim enemy or allies,[25] and the battle in a Pyrenean pass, and although the consequences of the French defeat form part of the *MR*, those details are not related to the previous tradition. The most significant component in all the previous narratives is the invasion of Spain by the Franks, later the French, with or without warning, which is also absent from the *MR*.[26] In a unique turn, Rodrigo doesn't repulse the Franks as they invade Spain, he leads an invasion of France. It may seem reasonable to suggest that the difference between repulsing an invasion of Spain by Charlemagne in a Pyrenean mountain pass and invading France is a matter of degrees, especially when both actions are based on a similar threat or demand. The difference is significant, however, when additional narrative sources are considered, and it becomes clear that the invasion episode is more than an escalation of a previous narrative tradition.[27]

The episode begins with the king declaring his inability to act after hearing a plea for resolution in an unrelated matter. Rodrigo's absence from the court has left the king uneasy, and he is then further burdened by the delivery of a letter from the king of France demanding tribute: "En esta querella llegó otro mandado./Cartas del rey de Françia e del emperador alemano,/cartas del patriarca e del papa romano,/que diesse tributo España a Françia, desde Aspa fasta en Santiago" ["In the midst of this plea another message arrived,/letters from the king of France and from the German emperor,/letters from the patriarch and the Roman pope,/that Spain pay tribute to France, from Aspe as far as Santiago"] (*Las Mocedades* vv. 804–7).[28] The demand for payment is met with bewilderment and anguished disbelief by the king. He sees his trans-Pyrenean rivals taking advantage of his youth and inexperience in order to impose an unprecedented demand on him "a mí veenme niño e sin sesso e vanme soberviando" ["they see me as a boy and without any sense and insist on demeaning me"] (v. 822). Rodrigo is summoned to the court, and the king charges him with the command of the armies of the five kings of Spain "que los çinco reys d'España quiero que anden por tu mano" ["for the five kings of Spain I want them to be led by your hand"] (v. 833).

Rodrigo is exhilarated by the opportunity to take action and immediately establishes an air of authority that will guide them both through the upcoming travails. Rodrigo interprets the demand for tribute as an opportunity, specifically an invitation to attack France and to plunder their wealth. In Rodrigo's interpretation of the decree, the French are not asking for tribute, they are sending riches (by providing a justification for an invasion), which the Spanish will gladly take from them. Rodrigo then orders the king to summon the armies of his kingdom from Aspe to Santiago (the same geographical reference employed in the letter) and swears to reach the very gates of Paris (vv. 837–43).

Rodrigo then leads the vanguard of the Spanish forces into France. The first battle pits his army, some three hundred mounted warriors, against the nineteen hundred men led by the count of Savoy. The two sides charge towards one another, and Rodrigo unhorses the count and takes him prisoner (bringing to mind the imprisonment of the "muy franco" count of Barcelona in the *Cantar*, v. 1068). As ransom for his freedom, the count hands over his only heir, his golden-haired, dark-eyed daughter, whom Rodrigo immediately hands over to his king, and in so doing instructs him to "¡Embarraganad a Francia!" (v. 1045), politely translated as "Make France your mistress!", but whose meaning leaves her somewhere between a whore and a concubine, an act meant to incite the French into renewing hostilities.

The king grants Rodrigo another nine hundred warriors, and he sets his camp before the army of the French. This time, however, he passes through the enemy camp alone to confront his enemies directly and manages to reach the gates of Paris. There he knocks on the gate and stops before the pope, calling out to the French and to the pope, demanding that they summon the Twelve Peers to do battle:

> Allí movió Ruy Díaz.
> Entre las tiendas de los françeses expoloneó al cavallo,
> e ferían los pies e la tierra iva temblando.
> En las puertas de París fue ferir con la mano,
> a pessar de françesses fue passar commo de cabo.
> Parósse ante'l papa, muy quedo estido,

"¿Qué es esso, françesses e papa romano?
Siempre oí dezir que Doze Pares avía en Françia, lidiadores, ¡llamadlos!
Si quesieren lidiar comigo, cavalguen muy privado."   (vv. 1096–104)

Then Ruy Díaz set out./Through the tents of the French he spurred his
horse,/and the hooves struck and the ground was shaking./The gates of
Paris he struck with his hand,/in spite of the French he got through as
before./He stopped before the pope, he stood very still,/"What is wrong,
Frenchmen and Roman pope?/I always heard that France had Twelve
Peers, fighters, call them!/If they want to fight me, have them mount up
immediately."

After an unsatisfactory response from the king of France, Rodrigo
replies, "Rey, vós e los Doce Pares de mí serés buscado" ["King, you
and the Twelve Peers will be sought out by me"] (v. 1110).

This aggressive stand by Rodrigo, first in the battle against the
count of Savoy, and now in his call to battle against the Twelve Peers
of France, far surpasses the incremental escalation evidenced in the
evolving exploits of Bernardo del Carpio. Once Rodrigo crossed the
Pyrenees into France and confronted his enemies on their soil, he broke
new ground. Since we would search in vain through history for a Spanish invasion of France, we must turn elsewhere to find a precedent for
this episode.

A similar call to battle forms the basis of a much more extensive episode in the French *chanson de geste, Fierabras* (c. 1190). Its eponymous
protagonist is a giant in stature and a fearless warrior. The son of Balan,
the Muslim emir of Spain, Fierabras led his father's armies in the sack-
ing of Rome, personally killed the pope, and retrieved the sacred relics
of Christ before returning to Spain. The Franks were called to come
to the aid of the Romans, but they arrived too late. They followed
the Muslim army to Spain in pursuit of the holy relics, and Fierabras,
enraged at their arrival on Spanish soil, seeks them out. When he spots
the enemy camp, he challenges the Franks to battle. It is his individual
quest against the French army and the call to the French warriors to do
battle that offer a parallel with the episode of Rodrigo challenging the
king of France before the gates of Paris:

A hautes vois s'escrie: 'Ahi! roi de Paris,
Envoie à moi jouster, mauvais couars falis,
De tes barons de France cels qui plus sont de pris,
Rollant et Ollivier, et s'I viegne Tierris,
Et Ogiers li Danois, qui tant par est hardis;
Ja n'en refuserai, par Mahom, jusqu'à .vi.

Et se nes envoiés ansi con j'ai requis,
Ains le vespre seras à ton tref assalis.
Ja ne m'en tornerai si seras desconfis;
Puis te taurai la teste au branc qui est forbis,
Rollant et Ollivier enmerrai je chaitis;
Mar passastes chà outré, mauvais couars poris.'   (*Fierabras*, vv. 79–90)

Ahoy there, king of Paris, you coward! Let me meet/The boldest of your
barons, the bravest of your breed – /Count Oliver and Roland and him
called Thierri/And Ogier, count of Denmark, whose valor is esteemed./I'll
take on half a dozen of your exalted peers!/If you refuse to send them or
fight against me here,/Then I shall come for you, Charles, before the night
is here,/And you will not escape me, but learn to taste defeat/Before I cut
your head off – one stroke is all I'll need – /And lead away your heroes to
Balan the emir!/You'll rue the day you landed, you reckless, feckless fiend!
                                          (*Fierabras and Floripas*, vv. 1588–98)

The settings and the expression are not an exact parallel, yet the challenge from Fierabras is close enough to the call to battle voiced by
Rodrigo to stand as a compelling case of influence.[29] Both Rodrigo and
Fierabras confront the French alone and directly challenge the Peers
to combat, whether all twelve or half a dozen of the best of all French
warriors.[30] This example of influence gains strength from other parallels between the two works, which I have explored in detail previously
("Charlemagne as a Creative Force" 39–42). Together, they help us to
understand the way in which a traditional narrative can incorporate
episodes from other traditions, in this case the French demand for submission and Fierabras's challenge to the Twelve Peers, across cultures
and languages, time and space, and adapt them in a way that makes
their otherness nearly imperceptible, certainly to the audience of the
time, and still for us today.

From the *Mocedades* back to the *Nota Emilianense*, the texts examined in this first chapter demonstrate how for well over three hundred
years (1070–1400), the legends surrounding Charlemagne's 778 invasion of Spain inspired poets and their audiences while challenging
the chroniclers who struggled to reconcile the different versions. The
heroes are reflections of one another, projecting in words and deeds
the responses of countless audiences to the legendary accounts of the
invasion of Spain by Charlemagne. French heroism is realized in the
virtuous fight against the Muslim enemy, whereas for the Spanish,
envisioned by the French as Muslims, their heroes are Christians who
first fight alongside Muslims in defending their common homeland,

and then take the fight to the French alone. In at least one version, these parallel tendencies seem to have led to a fruitful cross-pollination. Fierabras, the young Spanish Muslim protagonist of a French epic poem who fought the French heroically before being vanquished, converting to Christianity, and joining his former foes, became the model for the subsequent challenger of the Twelve Peers at the gates of Paris by the young Castilian warrior Rodrigo Díaz. This final episode provides only the most salient example of the convergence of the French and Spanish epic traditions spanning several centuries while having virtually no contact with the written record of the historical events that inspired them. Chroniclers tried to reign in the excesses of these legends, determined to reduce the rich bounty of the oral traditions that spawned them, to bend them to their own understanding of heroism and hierarchy, but they were no match for the imagination and self-renewing relevancy of a narrative tradition in continual evolution and nurtured by the sustained interaction between countless poets and audiences.

Chroniclers, in this case clerics writing history for royal patrons, seem particularly intent on erasing the impulses of the warrior heroes featured in oral narratives toward independent action and right-thinking, important attributes linking Bernardo del Carpio and the young Cid. This is true as well for the *Poema de Fernán González*, a *mester de clerecía* narration which reframes a traditional narrative on the heroic deeds of the Castilian count. Missing from that account, however, is the powerful confrontation between its Castilian hero and his liege lord, the king of León. We know that this confrontation exists as part of the traditional narrative because it is recreated in vibrant detail in the *Mocedades* (vv. 64–105). Here, freed from the cleric's censure, Fernán González challenges the authority of the king of León over the Castilians, mocking him as inferior and therefore unworthy of his elevated status. The eventual release from Leonese dominion gained by the initial defiance and subsequent latent cunning of the count is attained peacefully and celebrated in the poem, underlining the positive perception of his actions.

The narrative of Rodrigo, the young Cid, also defiant before his liege lord Fernando I, initially the count of Castile (1029), eventually king of León (1038), in the pursuit of his right-thinking intention to prove his mettle before submitting to marriage and to vassalage to his lord, also proves through his actions that the course he has chosen for himself is correct. In the final campaign of the narrative, Rodrigo is entrusted with the armies of all of Spain in their invasion of France to ensure that Spain remains independent of European rule. While the chronicle also recreates these events, Rodrigo is therein portrayed as a pliant and subservient vassal, certainly no epic hero, while the grandeur of his deeds attaches to the king, Fernando "par de emperador."

The next chapter will look more closely at these characterizations, especially the confrontations between vassal and lord, examined as a recurring motif in the Rodrigo narrative designed to produce an affective response in the audience, the struggle for independence as a unifying theme in the poem, and Rodrigo's penchant for speaking truth to power as an essential quality of his charismatic leadership.

Chapter Two

Affect and the Quest for Narrative Coherence

At any moment hundreds, perhaps thousands of stimuli impinge upon the human body and the body responds by infolding them all at once and registering them as an intensity. Affect is this intensity.

– Eric Shouse, "Feeling, Emotion, Affect"

Parrhesia, then, is linked to courage in the face of danger: it demands the courage to speak the truth in spite of some danger. And, in its extreme form, telling the truth takes place in the "game" of life or death.

– Michel Foucault, *Fearless Speech*

By far the majority of the critical attention given to the *Mocedades de Rodrigo* focuses on the coherence of the narrative.[1] Early readings of the poem understood it as a poorly preserved rite of initiation for the young protagonist, a ritualized coming-of-age story in which Rodrigo vowed to delay his marriage and service to the king until he had won five battlefield victories. Subsequent studies confirmed this interpretation by identifying thematic parallels between Rodrigo's first combat and his subsequent return to civil society and the Irish epic saga, *Táin Bó Cúailnge*, especially the initiation rite of its hero, Cú Chulainn. A poorly copied manuscript, an inattentive copyist, and a later prosaic clerical hand all contributed to the difficulty in reaching a consensus on just which battles should be counted among the five that Rodrigo vowed to win, or whether or not his vow was fulfilled before the final battle of the poem, Spain's invasion of France. Other ways of understanding progression in the poem were also advanced, such as the flowering of the alliance between Rodrigo and King Fernando, or the melding of the public and the private spheres in a triumphal allegiance that benefits king and vassal. Finally, a few readings eschew the search for cohesion

and posit a series of episodes linked by a single protagonist, or a preference for a compositional principle based on fragmentation and heterogeneous actors.

This chapter takes note of previous scholarship on the lack of narrative cohesion in the text and proposes a reading of the poem that
acknowledges the imperfections of the extant text but nevertheless recognizes a unifying theme, a strong-willed but exemplary protagonist
throughout, and a progression in which Rodrigo sets the rules that at
first estrange him from others, queering him, so to speak, but eventually lead to an absolute trust in his counsel and a recognition of his ability to forge powerful alliances for a unified purpose. This progression
plays out through a series of affective encounters in which the deep
humanity of the poem's principal protagonists is on full display. We see
them in moments of high pathos, when they are literally beside themselves, and this vulnerability, these transcendent moments, produce a
deeper understanding and create the psychic space that leads to new
and fruitful allegiances.

One way to appreciate the importance to scholars of the identification
of a unifying theme in the *Mocedades* is by reviewing previous scholarship on the poem's perceived incoherence, based on a select group of
insightful and well-reasoned interpretations. Montgomery imagines a
compiler of the poem, not an author in any sense that would resonate
with us today. His compiler knew a biography of the young Cid that
included specific genealogical information, names, and other details,
some fairly extensive passages of superior quality, along with others
that were little more than rudimentary ballads. As these passages were
brought together, the compiler could add others of his own confection
with a very basic knowledge of epic verse, in this case simple end-
rhyme. The compiler would also feel free to include a legendary history of the diocese of Palencia and to exclude the historical conquest of
Coimbra by Fernando I, as part of the creative process of an evolving,
vibrant poetic tradition ("Las *MR* y los romances" 132–3). The disparate literary quality of the extant text leads Montgomery to imagine a
process in which some of the finer passages were recreated over time as
ballads, independently of the longer narrative. The more frequent repetition among diverse audiences would have served to improve these
passages, and thus improved, they were later re-incorporated into the
extant narrative (120–1). And even though the traces of this creative
process are more evident in the *Mocedades* than in other Spanish epics,
Montgomery assumes a similar process for the Spanish epic in general,
citing a number of thematic and stylistic inconsistencies in the vener-
able *Cantar* (133).[2]

Montaner also sees the extant poem as imperfect in its coherence. He envisions an author who refined and added material of his own confection to create a unified structure for what was previously a body of pre-existing heterogeneous legendary material on the young Cid ("La *Gesta*" 432, 434). Montaner imagines an early narrative on Rodrigo's youthful deeds, a now lost *gesta*, previous to the extant text, conceived uniformly and organized via a bipartite structure: the first portion including Rodrigo's betrothal and ending with his vow to win five pitched battles; the second portion comprising those five battles (and his marriage). The poem's narrative inconsistency that Montgomery associates with the uneven quality of the pre-existing materials, Montaner attributes to the ideological implications of the last of Rodrigo's five battles, the fabulous Spanish invasion of France, that by virtue of its importance from the perspective of thirteenth-century political philosophy, simply overwhelmed the structural role of Rodrigo's vow ("La *Gesta*" 441).

Funes concurs with Montgomery and Montaner that the poem was compiled from passages that had developed independently of a larger narrative and invokes it as an explanation for the ideological inconsistencies and heterogeneous content observed in the poem (liii–lx). Unlike Montgomery, Funes attributes the poem's inconsistencies to a compositional principle ("principio constructivo") unique to this epic poem (l). The audience he imagines for the poem, able to process and enjoy what Funes sees as an incoherent narrative, must have been accepting of a new compositional principle, which he terms "romancístico" ("balladic"), based on a familiarity with the shorter narrative structure of ballads (l). In his final analysis of this process, Funes describes a poem in which "la escena se impone al relato ... y solo importa el despliegue de la contienda verbal" ["the scene imposes itself onto the story ... and only the unfolding of the verbal conflict matters"], a poem that celebrates a "peculiar heroicidad de las palabras" ["a peculiar heroism of words"] (lxii). Funes also identifies an ideological principle that favours rebellious heroes in the selection of passages that comprise the poem (lviii–lx). Marta Lacomba adopts Funes's argument that the narrative does not proceed in a linear fashion but is more analogical in its construction (para. 4), adding the concept of "retroalimentación," an incremental process in which the protagonists rightfully challenge authority (para. 33). Through this process, the narrative reinforces the notion of justified intransigence in a way that prompts the reader to reach the same conclusion.[3]

The hybrid nature of the text and the uneven quality of many of its passages, including some of the best in epic expression along with others that are more akin to comic books (Montgomery, "Some Singular Passages" 123–6, 132), has made it difficult for scholars to imagine a single author or audience for the poem. Yet there is a clear thematic cohesion based on the depiction of the will to independence and desire for self-rule of the early Castilians, initially from León (Laín Calvo and Nuño Rasura; Fernán González), then from royal authority (Diego Laínez and Rodrigo), and finally from France and the other European powers (King Fernando and Rodrigo), as well as the diocese of Palencia from other claimants (Bernardo and Miro). The fight for independence and self-determination begins with the two early lords ["alcaldes"] of Castile, the magnates Nuño Rasura and Laín Calvo (vv. 12–16), who ruled Castile in service to the distant king of León. The final battle of the poem is undertaken by the descendants of these two lords, King Fernando and Rodrigo, who join forces to punish the king of France and other European powers for their temerity in demanding that Spain pay them tribute. This view of Castilian history is a contrivance enabled by the author of the poem.[4] It is not substantiated by historical evidence or previous literary tradition, and since the poem is composed of disparate, heterogeneous passages, we should look to the arc of history that the poem presents as perhaps the most significant contribution of the poem's author.

There is another way in which the poem shows narrative coherence. The encounters between the narrative's main protagonists feature powerful affective responses such as surprise, fear, or anger, and these responses then create a psychic space, a vulnerability perhaps, that leads to transcendent agreements or new allegiances. These encounters also take place in parts of the narrative in which Rodrigo is not featured, as in the narration of the deeds of the count of Castile, Fernán González, an early ancestor of King Fernando, and to a lesser degree in the narration of the fight for the self-determination of the diocese of Palencia. As we shall soon see, they are a feature of the poem throughout, and another way to understand its coherence, in this case, aesthetic.

This focus on the encounters between the poem's main protagonists has previously led to their identification as a defining characteristic of the compositional principle of the poem, although with significant differences in emphasis. Earlier descriptions of the episodic nature of the poem suggest an ideological coherence, based on "una visión social uniforme en torno a la consideración armónica de las relaciones entre la nobleza y la monarquía, bajo la éjida de ésta" ["a uniform social vision centred on the harmonious conception of the relations between nobility and monarchy, under the aegis of the latter"] (Montaner, "La *Gesta*" 440, restated 441) or, to the contrary, a significant recurrence of episodes that feature "una exaltación de la rebeldía o del enfrentamiento ante una figura de autoridad o de poder superior" ["a celebration of rebelliousness or of confrontation with an authority figure or someone with more power"] (Funes xlviii; adopted and reexamined in Lacomba). In what follows, the detailed analysis of these principal encounters will serve to provide a more nuanced understanding of them and a fuller appreciation of their role in the thematic and aesthetic coherence of the narrative.

There are of course many episodes from which to choose, but in order to emphasize the coherence of the entirety of the poem, this analysis will begin by examining passages that are not directly related to Rodrigo's youth, namely those found in its first 345 verses (from a total of 1,225 verses). The poem begins with brief mentions of the earliest Castilians, Laín Calvo and Nuño Rasura, the two leaders ("alcaldes") responsible for defending Castile in the service of the king of León. This arrangement allowed for one leader to remain in Castile when the king called his Castilian surrogate to court (vv. 12–16). As the narration moves toward the story of Fernán González, the count celebrated for freeing Castile from its vassalage to the kingdom of León (v. 103), some jarring details about his ancestors are offered: Nuño Rasura's son, Gonzalo Nuñez, was "malo e traviesso" ["evil and malicious"] such that "quíssolo el padre matar" ["his father wanted to kill him"] (v. 22); his future wife, the daughter of King Sancho Ramírez of Navarra, doña Aldara Sánchez, "andava mala mugier con los moros" ["lived sinfully among the Moors"] (v. 26); of their three sons, the first two "non valieron nada" ["were useless"] (v. 30); Fernán Gonçález, the third son, was captured by King Sancho Ordóñez de Navarra "por engaño" ["through deceit"] (v. 36); in his escape he was aided by the sister of the king, doña Costança, who "tomólo la infanta a sus cuestas" ["carried him on her back"] (v. 40); an archpriest spies them and demands that doña Costança "le fiziesse amor de su cuerpo" ["make love to him with her body"] (v. 43), or "los descobriría" ["he would report them"] (v. 42); but while doña Costança embraces her aspirational violator, the count "matólo con el su cochillo mismo del açipreste" ["killed him with the archpriest's own knife"] (v. 46).

These passages are as much a part of the narrative as the later, more detailed episodes related to Rodrigo, since they reference the ancestors of King Fernando (Nuño Rasura, one of two foundational Castilian leaders) and Rodrigo (Laín Calvo). Yet they don't conform to the overall understanding of the poem's essence as a series of "contienda verbal" ["verbal confrontations"] (Funes xlix), nor do they portray anything like a "consideración armónica de las relaciones entre la nobleza y la monarquía" ["harmonious conception of the relations between nobility and monarchy"] (Montaner, "La *Gesta*" 440), nor are they reminiscent of balladic compositions, as Montgomery would have it. In fact, these lines have no end-rhyme but are organized through anaphora, in this case the repetition of "e(t)" ["and"], although here it is a mnemonic device, not employed for poetic effect but as an aid to oral composition (Bailey, *The Poetics of Speech* 111–15). A link between this passage and later episodes that does seem relevant is the genealogical foundation of the two main protagonists and a penchant for lurid or shocking revelations that would likely prod the audience into reconsidering their conception of heroic attributes and conduct.

The author soon switches his compositional mode to end-rhyme, so we might expect to begin to see passages more in line with the characterization of the poem made by Montgomery and Funes, that is, of passages that most likely circulated independently of the poem in a balladic state, improving their expression, before being reintegrated into the extant text (Montgomery, "Las *MR* y los romances" 120–1; Funes l–li). In fact, the episode in which Fernán González confronts Alfonso, the king of León, and comes away as the lord of Castile freed from its vassalage to León, is one of several that Funes identifies as emblematic of the compositional process for the poem, one of three "realizaciones plenas" ["full realizations"] of what he terms an "escena matriz" ["core scene"] (xlix). These paradigmatic scenes are singled out because they portray a "contienda verbal entre una figura de autoridad y una figura de rebeldía: la figura de autoridad convoca a un encuentro, la figura de rebeldía acude a ese encuentro, en el que se desarrolla una contienda verbal que culmina con el desacuerdo o la ruptura y la preeminencia de la figura de rebeldía" ["a verbal confrontation between a figure of authority and a rebellious figure: the authority figure calls a meeting, the rebellious figure accedes to the meeting, in which a verbal confrontation takes place that culminates in disagreement or in rupture and the preeminence of the rebellious figure"] (Funes xlix).

In the examination of this particular scene, it seems relevant to point out that Fernán González is not portrayed as a rebellious figure, nor does any kind of "rupture" take place. As the scene begins, the king calls Fernán González to court, "e fue el conde muy pagado" ["and the count went happily"] (v. 71), and so "very pleased" to be going to court, and again, "Cavalgó el conde commo omne tan lozano" ["the count rode as a very proud man"] (v. 72). Further along, the king expresses wonder at how the count dares to not respond when he is called to court in service to the king, "de non me venir a mis cortes nin me bessar la mano" ["to not come to my courts or kiss my hand"] (v. 77), for Castile was always a tributary to León and that "León es regno e Castilla es condado" ["León is a kingdom and Castile is a county"] (vv. 78–9). The count replies that the king is clearly mistaken "mucho andades en vano" (v. 80), since his mount is a heavy mule "buena mula gruessa," while the count is on a good horse "buen cavallo" (v. 81). The count then expresses his amazement that he has allowed the king to treat him as a vassal, when he is lord of Castile "en aver señor Castilla y pedirle vós tributario" (v. 83). This disagreement will be decided in the king's court. In their subsequent meeting the king covets the count's hawk and horse, which the count agrees to sell to him at compounding interest "al gallarín ge lo vendió el conde" (v. 91). The payment isn't made promptly, the interest grows, and the count demands payment as a condition for returning to the king's call to court. Finally, the king concedes that he can't make the payment and in recompense Castile is released from its vassalage to the king of León (vv. 98–103).

Although the count does refuse to acknowledge any Castilian tributary status before the king of León, there is no specific instance in which the count rebels against the king. The liberation of Castile from vassalage to León is accomplished through a legal transaction, the sale of the count's hawk and horse. The count is said to be pleased with his good fortune in being able to free Castile from Leonese overlordship (v. 102). In this sense, then, Fernán González is not so much a "figura de rebeldía" as a confident and right-thinking vassal.

Fernán González and his ancestors are not described as great warriors or rebellious vassals. The deeds for which they are memorialized retain something more akin to wonder or surprise, memorable because they are unusual and, in fact, seem very distant from anything we might wish to term "epic." What they do communicate is the unexpected, a surprising turn, that makes them memorable and thus retainable. The author of the poem includes them as part of the ancestral genealogy of Fernando I, the co-protagonist of Rodrigo's deeds. The episodes that relate the deeds of Fernán González are more extensive and detailed than the material dedicated to his ancestors and, as such, indicate a higher degree of popularity (vv. 31–105). This popularity is also verifiable in the extensive narration of his deeds in the *PFG* and subsequently in the Alfonsine and post-Alfonsine chronicles, the latter beginning with the *Crónica de Castilla*. In these texts a number of battles are narrated, whereas in the *Mocedades* Fernán González is not portrayed in battle; his most memorable actions are verbal in nature. This characterization also applies to the deeds of Rodrigo in the poem, in which verbal confrontation merits more attention than actual fighting (following Funes 1).

Rodrigo's vow to win five pitched battles before consummating his marriage or kissing the king's hand in fealty may well have been more of a defining theme in an earlier version of the narrative. In an apparent echo of the young Rodrigo's vow, the mature Cid is said to have achieved the challenge he set for himself ("e fizo çinco lides campales e todas las arrancó," *Cantar*, v. 1333). The extant text, however, is a bit more muddled in the matter. The pitched battles that Rodrigo does undertake do not add up to five and as a result, like-minded scholars have been unable to agree on which battles to count (reviewed by Funes xl–xliii). Another problem with this reading of the poem is that the process should culminate with the consummation of Rodrigo's marriage to Ximena, yet no marriage takes place in the poem. In fact, we cannot be sure of how the poem concludes, since the manuscript ends abruptly while leaving a few final folios blank.[5]

What is clearly conveyed in the poem is Rodrigo's willingness to fight for self-determination, at first on behalf of his family, then for himself, and finally, once the male members of his family have been killed in battle, on behalf of the king for a threatened Spain ("Esto lo aconsejó por el buen rey don Fernando," v. 746). Rodrigo never fails to demonstrate an instinctive aggression towards his enemies, a fearless embrace of battle, and disdain for compromise or negotiation. These attributes are not exclusive to youth, and they are present in the portrayal of Rodrigo from beginning to end, so they don't really serve any concept of progression or maturation that scholars have searched for in the poem.

A theme that does provide a sense of progression in the poem is the king's increasing awareness of Rodrigo's value as an ally. His victories in battle and his willingness to fight the king's enemies when the king's own vassals demur or, in the case of the traitorous counts of Castile, actively scheme against him, make Rodrigo especially valuable to the king. Thus, Rodrigo's star does rise in the poem, over time, as the king manages to gain his cooperation in confronting the problems he faces and is unable to resolve without him. At the same time, Rodrigo's successes continue to accrue due to his natural aggression, his determination to win battles, and his unwillingness to compromise, producing a realignment of loyalties in his favour. His personal traits, along with his Christian charity, confer upon Rodrigo God's favour and render him invincible, from his first battle to his last.

Understanding the poem as a process of maturation, a coming of age, is misleading, since it takes away from an appreciation of Rodrigo's inherently aggressive characteristics and his highly personalized mode of confronting and confounding his allies and enemies, attributes that are on display throughout the poem. In dialogues with his allies, his father, the king, and his nephew (Pero Mudo), Rodrigo speaks truth to power or simply truth in a direct and unvarnished manner. There is also a kind of boldness to Rodrigo's aggression and in the humiliation of his enemies, and this boldness, this excess, I believe, represents an important and irreducible dimension of the poem's appeal and import (following Christensen 100). This appeal is so strong that it overwhelms and ultimately displaces any inclination the author may have had in reproducing or creating anew the structure of a traditional narrative, focusing on the scenes of Rodrigo's excess to recall and celebrate.

Essentially, all of Rodrigo's encounters can be understood in this way, as compelling in their aggressiveness or his willingness to speak truth to power. His frank confrontations with figures of authority elicit surprise as we witness his efforts to chart his own course, to maintain at first his own independence, and subsequently the sovereignty of Castile. Rodrigo does win over detractors through his words and his actions, but unlike other Spanish epic poems such as the *Cid* or the *Fernán González*, it is difficult to point to specific moments in the narrative that might be considered transitional. All of the scenes of Rodrigo's youth are of strife and conflict, as he is in constant movement and unending confrontation. In this poem, no one rests. There are incidents that produce fear in Rodrigo's enemies, wonder and admiration in his allies, and befuddlement in the king when Rodrigo refuses to bow to his authority. Ximena as well, in the brief time she is given in the poem, first perplexes and then surprises her audience by her demands in staking out a future for herself. The actors in these scenes are portrayed as either surprising others or being surprised, aggressive or fearful, bold or unable to act, with depictions that might be best understood as affective, that is, physical responses linked to basic emotions, which minimally include fear, anger, disgust, joy, sadness, and surprise.

There is some discord in scholarship regarding theories of affect, in that affects can be understood as occurring intentionally, governed by our beliefs, cognitions, and desires, or non-intentionally, occurring independently of intention or meaning, each one manifesting itself "in distinct physiological-autonomic and behavioural patterns of response, especially in characteristic facial expressions" (Leys 438). This distinction is not the focus of the present study, but it may nevertheless be useful to keep in mind as we explore the representation of affect in the poem.

Some of the affective responses in the poem are linked to specific causes, although not all are clearly attributed. Their examination should help us better appreciate the role of affect in the narrative, provide insights into the compelling nature of certain scenes, and may even help explain the will to preserve the poem in writing. In addition, the scenes that most clearly convey affective responses are also the instances in which Rodrigo speaks unvarnished truth, mostly to his king, but also to his allies and family members. Their examination is crucial to this chapter, as they challenge our expectations regarding the portrayal of relationships between persons of highest authority, Rodrigo's father, the king, the pope, etc., and those who are of lower social rank or station, such as the young Rodrigo. These are also the scenes that have led scholars to brand the young Rodrigo a rebel (reviewed and synthesized in Funes xlviii–xlix), or at the very least as "arrogant and uncouth" (Lacarra Lanz 469). In fact, and to the contrary, Rodrigo seems to present as a model of exemplary behaviour and reason, especially in comparison to his interlocutors.[6] These encounters undoubtedly resonated with emotion and meaning for the poem's author and for the audiences that helped mould them over time. The scenes of affective response and Rodrigo's boldness and straight talk in his quest for autonomy for himself and later for Castile produce highly compelling scenes. It is reasonable to assume that their emotional charge simply overwhelmed the relevance of the rite of passage on which Rodrigo's youthful deeds were at one time structured. The affective power of these compelling encounters between Rodrigo and his enemies and allies produced a kind of interlude in the narration of his deeds, a focus not on the deed itself but on the exchanges portrayed in their narration, and most likely engendered a sense of urgency for author and audience in moving from one charged encounter to the next.

In the first episode to be examined, Rodrigo has killed Count don Gómez de Gormaz and captured his two sons, leaving his daughter Ximena without her father and brothers, the males on whom the household likely depends. Her first act of restitution is to take it upon herself, the youngest of the count's daughters, to demand the release of her brothers from captivity. For this she leads her sisters to Vivar, to Rodrigo and his father:

> Salen de Gormaz e vanse para Bivar.
> Violas venir don Diego e a reçebirlas sale,
> "¿D'ónde son aquestas freiras, que algo me vienen demandar?"
> "Dezirvos hemos, Señor, que non avemos por qué vos lo negar.
> Fijas somos del conde don Gormaz, e vós le mandastes matar,
> prissístesnos los hermanos e tenédeslos acá,
> e nós mugieres somos, que non ay quién nos anpare."
> Essas oras dixo don Diego, "Non devedes a mí culpar,
> peditlas a Rodrigo, si vos las quesiere dar,

prométolo yo a Cristus, a mí non me puede pessar."
Aquesto oyó Rodrigo, comenzó de fablar,
"Mal fezistes, señor, de vós negar la verdat,
que yo seré vuestro fijo e seré de mi madre.
Parat mientes al mundo, señor, por caridat,
non han culpa las fijas por lo que fizo el padre.
Datles a sus hermanos, que muy menester los han,
contra estas dueñas mesura devedes catar."
Allí dixo don Diego, "Fijo, mandátgelos dar."
Sueltan los hermanos, a las dueñas los dan. (vv. 388–406)

They leave Gormaz and go to Vivar./don Diego saw them coming and went out to receive them,/"Where are these sisters from, that come to demand something of me?"/"We will tell you, Sire, we have no reason to deny it./We are the daughters of Count don Gormaz, and you ordered him killed,/you captured our brothers and you are holding them here,/and we are women, there is no one to protect us."/Then don Diego said, "You should not blame me,/ask Rodrigo for them, if he wants to give them to you,/I swear to God, it will not bother me."/Rodrigo heard this, he began to speak,/"You did wrong, Sire, in denying the truth,/and I will respond as your son and my mother's son (as who I am)./Think about how the world works, Sire, for heaven's sake,/the daughters are not to blame for what their father did./Give them their brothers, for they have great need of them,/you should show compassion for these ladies."/Then don Diego said, "Son, order them released."/They free the brothers, they give them to the ladies.

Ximena's plea is reasonable, as is Rodrigo's response. He chides his father for being evasive and then gives him a lesson in clear thinking and in charity – not blaming the daughters for their father's aggression and recognizing the legitimate need they have for their brothers. In this confrontation, as in subsequent encounters between Rodrigo and his allies, Rodrigo is reasonable and speaks a clear-eyed version of the truth. His candor, in fact, is surprising, and his father immediately acknowledges this point by conceding his authority (vv. 405–6). Rodrigo's response must have impressed Ximena as well, for not long after this exchange she asks to be married to Rodrigo.

Rodrigo's rebuke of his father's deflection of responsibility for the capture of Ximena's brothers was most likely noted by the audience of the poem as a challenge to paternal authority. In a rigidly hierarchical society, we can imagine the exchange evoking surprise in the audience, making it memorable and compelling, qualities that would ensure the episode being recalled in later renditions of the poem. One of the frustrating characteristics of the poem for the modern reader is the near absence of metacommentary. In very few instances do the protagonists of the poem reflect on their actions or the actions of others, nor does the poet comment on the actions of the protagonists. In this instance the lack of a response from Rodrigo's father to the assertiveness of his son leaves us without a full sense of the episode's affective impact.

If this exchange were the only one in which Rodrigo challenges authority, we would rightly limit our appreciation of the episode to its use of affect as an aesthetic principle. Rodrigo's rebuke might initially come across as more of a suggestion than a challenge, an effort to be included in the decision-making process of the family, to establish a form of proto democracy for these foundational Castilians. But this is not the first or the last example of challenges by Rodrigo to figures of authority in the poem, starting within the family, progressing to the king's court, to the king himself, and ultimately escalating to world rulers.[7] For this reason and although this episode by itself is not conclusive, in the context of the fuller narrative Rodrigo's rebuke provides an early glimpse of a defining characteristic of the poem's protagonist, one that will become more pronounced and impossible to ignore as the poem progresses, his role as a *parrhesiastes*, as one who speaks truth to power.[8]

Although we can establish a correspondence between Rodrigo's truth-telling and Foucault's explication of the concept of truth-telling as drawn from his analysis of two tragedies by Euripides, it is highly unlikely that the author of the *MR*, his audience, or the oral tradition that nurtured the Rodrigo narrative would have any knowledge of those ancient works. Nevertheless, from their origins in the Bernardo story examined earlier, as well as its corollary in the Fernán González narrative, these epic protagonists are celebrated for holding to account authority figures who show themselves to be incapable or unwilling to justify their status through right action. In a parallel fashion to the ancient tragedies of Euripedes, the *Mocedades* also creates literary fantasies based on the willingness of its protagonist to speak truth to power.[9]

In support of the leveraging of Foucault's work on *parrhesia* as a means to delve deeper into the social dynamic portrayed in the *Mocedades*, we may look to a recent study on Geoffrey Chaucer that evinces the ways in which the author of *The Canterbury Tales* was intrigued by the prospect of creating "fictional worlds held together by a desire for and anxiety about *parrhesia*" (Megna 32). Much like the pre-existing material that was used to compose the *Mocedades*, two of the three *Tales* examined in Megna's study, *The Second Nun's Tale* and *The Tale of Melibee* circulated independently prior to their incorporation by Chaucer into his work (Megna 32, 35), suggesting that they sparked the author's interest in portraying *parrhesia* more fully in *The Canterbury Tales*. The echoes of the heroic narratives of Bernardo del Carpio, Fernán González, Fierabras, and Cú Chulainn in the *Mocedades* narrative suggest that Rodrigo's portrayal as a *parrhesiastes* predated its composition and that the emotional charge of the disruptive nature of Rodrigo as truth-teller was an important factor in the forging of this literary work. It is also likely that its composition was part of an effort to promote a practice of fearless speech as an antidote to the beleaguered and ineffectual Castilian monarchy during the troubled minorities of Fernando IV and of Alfonso IV. This time frame seems especially apt for the creation of an account of the reign of Fernando I that could compete with the *Crónica de Castilla*, one in which something like *parrhesia* would guide the young monarchs in making better decisions and taking more forceful actions.[10]

Returning to the narrative with confidence in the relevance of Foucault's findings to the *Mocedades*, Rodrigo's rebuke of his father, in which he is "an equal or subordinate in the social hierarchy," provides an example of positive *parrhesia* (Megna 31). This positive sense entails five characteristics (Foucault 11–20; summarized in Megna 31), all of which are present in the episode, but especially and perhaps most significantly for its association with affect is the risk that Rodrigo takes on by "the fact that the said truth is capable of hurting or angering the *interlocutor*" (Foucault 17). Rodrigo's rebuke to his father surely surprises and likely angers him. The audience, alert to the implications of Rodrigo's undermining of parental authority, would likely respond with surprise and perhaps with dread of the consequences for Rodrigo.

Delving deeper into the consideration of Rodrigo's challenge to his father's authority, we might ask ourselves what purpose it serves. What does Rodrigo gain by challenging his father in this way? As evidenced by the exchange and its outcome, a more just result for Ximena and her sisters. The brothers are returned to their sisters because, as Rodrigo points out, the sisters are not to blame for their father's transgressions, and they need their brothers to look after them. Initially at least, justice is accorded the sisters through Rodrigo's intervention. We might expect an equally altruistic response from the brothers, perhaps leading to a peaceful end to a bloody rivalry and in this way Rodrigo's righteous act would be preserved as exemplary.

Yet, upon their release, the brothers show no sign of recognizing or honouring Rodrigo's risky intervention. The brothers immediately begin planning a raid under the cover of darkness to burn down the Laínez family property in retaliation for the death of their father (vv. 407–9). This turn of events affords Ximena, the youngest of the siblings, an opportunity to assume her own leadership, as she counsels her brothers to allow her to obtain redress from the king. Ximena's challenge to

her older brothers' role as keepers of the family and its collective honour
is even more audacious than Rodrigo's rebuke of his father. Ximena had
induced Rodrigo's altruistic response by depicting herself and her sisters as dependent on their brothers for their well-being: "prissístesnos
los hermanos e tenédeslos acá,/e nós mugieres somos, que non ay quién
nos anpare" ["you captured our brothers and you are holding them
here,/and we are women, there is no one to protect us"] (vv. 393–4).
Now it seems, she is willing to challenge the authority of her brothers
by positioning herself as the agent best equipped to guarantee the prosperity of her family. Ximena is no longer a helpless victim.

In her audience with the king, Ximena's initial demand is for justice,
a reckoning for Rodrigo as the one responsible for her loss (vv. 414–23).
Again, this is a reasonable request that elicits no surprise from the
king. He is reluctant to act, to do the right thing, since he fears a violent
response from the Castilians to any imposition of his authority on them
(vv. 424–6). Ximena then comes up with a solution for the irresolute
king, and it is not what he or anyone else could have expected from this
self-professed victim of violence.

> Quando lo oyó Ximena Gómez, las manos le fue bessar,
> "Merçed," dixo, "Señor, non lo tengades a mal,
> mostrarvos he assosegar a Castilla e a los reinos otro tal.
> Datme a Rodrigo por marido, aquel que mató a mi padre."   (vv. 427–30)

> When Ximena Gómez heard this, she kissed his hands,/"If you please," she
> said, "Sire, don't let this worry you,/I'll show you how to pacify Castile,
> and your kingdoms as well./Give me Rodrigo for my husband, the one
> who killed my father."

The response from the young king is stunned silence, while his tutor
expresses his own surprise as disbelief that such a gift should have been
handed to the king in the form of a request, ostensibly freeing him from
having to confront a difficult choice between his duty to serve justice
and his fear of aggrieving the Castilians. He counsels the king to act
quickly, presumably before Ximena comes to her senses and changes
her mind, demonstrating that his disbelief is still active.

> Quando aquesto oyó el conde don Ossorio, amo del rey don Fernando,
> tomó el rey por las manos e aparte iva sacallo,
> "Señor, ¿qué vos semeja?, ¡qué don vos ha demandado!
> Mucho lo devedes agradeçer al Padre apoderado.
> Señor, enbiat por Rodrigo e por su padre privado."   (vv. 431–5)

When Count don Osorio heard this, tutor to King don Fernando,/he took the king by the hand and drew him aside,/"Sire, what do you think? What a gift she has requested of you! (Her request is a gift to you!)/You should truly thank the almighty Father./Sire, send for Rodrigo and for his father immediately."

The messenger is sent, but when the message is received by Rodrigo's father, he misinterprets it by incorrectly assuming that the news the letter brings is a ruse by the king and that his true intention is to kill them in retaliation for the death of the count. In counselling his son, he warns him that kings are to be considered their mortal enemies.

> Don Diego cató las cartas e ovo la color mudado,
> sospechó que por la muerte del conde quería el rey matarlo.
> "Oítme," dixo, "mi fijo, mientes catedes acae,
> témome de aquestas cartas que andan con falsedat,
> e d'esto los reys muy malas costumbres han.
> Al rey que vós servides, servillo muy sin arte,
> assí vós aguardat d'él commo de enemigo mortal."　　　　　(vv. 443–9)

Don Diego looked over the letters and his face flushed,/he suspected that for the death of the count the king wanted to kill him./"Hear me," he said, "My son, take a look at this,/I am fearful of these letters that are full of lies,/for in these matters kings have very evil ways./Any king you serve, serve him without trickery,/and be as wary of him as of a mortal enemy."

Following this advice, Rodrigo and his father naturally plan to arrive at the king's court fully armed. They are wrong in their assumption about the king's intentions of course, but their response is rational since a death sentence is just what they might expect as punishment for having killed the king's count. We don't know the content of the letter sent to don Diego, but if it does indeed communicate the king's intention to marry Rodrigo to Ximena, to raise Rodrigo up socially ("será aína Rodrigo encimado" v. 442), the incredulous response from don Diego and Rodrigo is another way to affirm the surprising nature of Ximena's request to take Rodrigo as her husband.

When the Castilians arrive at the king's court, still believing that the king plans to kill them, they are naturally equipped for battle. But it is Rodrigo's visage that shocks and unsettles the courtiers and the king. The narrator explains their reaction after describing how the courtiers all ran from the sight of him, thus rationalizing the fear Rodrigo provoked in them.

Irado va contra la corte do está el buen rey don Fernando,
todos dizen, "Ahé'l que mató al conde loçano."
Quando Rodrigo bolvió los ojos, todos ivan derramando.
Avién muy grant pavor d'él, e muy grande espanto.   (vv. 472–5)

He moves angrily towards the court of the good king don Fernando,/they
all say, "He's the one who killed the brave count."/When Rodrigo turned to
look at them, they all scattered./They were all very afraid of him and filled
with terror.

There is no description of Rodrigo's visage that might justify the flight of
the king's courtiers, all grown men, among them surely seasoned warriors, counts and royal counsellors. Yet their reaction is clearly affective (a
physical response to fear, intentional or not), linked to the expression on
Rodrigo's face (or in his eyes) when he turns to confront them ("Rodrigo
volvió los ojos" [v. 474], literally: "he turned his eyes"). Although the
courtiers may not have cognitively processed their response to Rodrigo's frightful visage, their response may have been unintentional, the
narrator makes the connection for the sake of narrative coherence.

Rodrigo's frightful appearance, probably best explained as an aggressive response to the threat of death that he and his father had assumed
awaited them at the king's court, and then revived when the couriers
commented on his role in the count's death, is portrayed as linked to
his facial expression, or through his eyes. Rodrigo's transformation
was linked by Montgomery to the "furia guerrera" that manifests in Cú
Chulainn, the young protagonist of the Irish epic saga *Táin Bó Cúailnge*
("*Las MR* y el *Táin Bó Cúailnge*" 42–3). In that narrative Cú Chulainn
does indeed present a frightful prospect as he returns from battle and
threatens to spill the blood of his clansmen assembled in the fort, unless
a man is sent out to fight him. To subdue his fury, the women of Emain,
including the queen, are sent out to confront him, baring their breasts
to him. The queen states, "These are the warriors you must take on
today," at which Cú Chulainn hides his face and is taken hold of by the
bare-breasted women and subdued (Carson 50). In essence, the young
warrior can defeat any man or beast, but he is no match for exposed
women.

Rodrigo is also represented as threatening the king when, as he bows
to kiss the king's hand, his broadsword slips into view. The king, recoil-
ing in fear ("fue mal espantado" v. 479), demands that Rodrigo, whom
he compares to the devil ("esse pecado" v. 480), be removed. As with
the king's assembled court in the *Táin*, there is extreme consternation
at the prospect of impending violence. This prompts the king to call

for Ximena to be brought out: "Dadme vós acá esss donçella, despos-saremos este lozano" (v. 485), for betrothal to Rodrigo. Ximena does not bare her breasts to Rodrigo, but she does subdue him through the impo-sition of marriage, which led Montgomery to describe her as a "femme impudique" ("Horatius 547).[11] Rodrigo manages to save face to some degree in attenuating his involuntary compliance by vowing to win five pitched battles before consummating his marriage, or kissing the king's hand, a sign of confirmed vassalage (vv. 490–5).

It is reasonable to see Rodrigo's response as rebelliousness towards the king. The royal chroniclers who put the narrative to prose were cer-tainly not inclined to acknowledge any agency on the part of Rodrigo, leading them to somewhat improbably portray Rodrigo as express-ing gratitude to the king for the imposition of marriage: "Et Rodrigo, quando esto oyó, plógol' mucho, et dixo al rey que faría su mandado en esto e en todas otras cosas que le él mandasse" ["And Rodrigo, when he heard this, it truly pleased him, and he told the king that he would obey him in this and all things that he might demand of him"] (*CC*, "Fernando I el Magno" para. 18; chap. 4). Another way to understand Rodrigo's response, his vow to win five pitched battles before submit-ting to marriage, is to see it as a reasonable reaction to a course of action that is premature and as such bound to hinder his growth as a warrior and as a productive member of society. If we recall the infantes de Car-rión and their immature and ultimately unmanly behaviour in the *Can-tar de mio Cid*, recalling that they were married before they had proven themselves in battle, we might agree that Rodrigo is right to postpone his marriage until he has established himself as a legitimate warrior (Montgomery, *Medieval Spanish Epic* 42). The postponement of his mar-riage and his obligation to serve the king until he has acquired the expe-rience and the status necessary to carry out these functions properly seems to be a very rational and even respectful response to the sudden and entirely unexpected imposition of the responsibilities of marriage and vassalage.

Rodrigo's agency is limited in this episode since he is compelled to accept the marriage dictate of the king, but by postponing the consummation of his marriage, he is able to retain a modicum of independence. The fear-some visage that arrived at court and sent fear through the hearts of the assembled warriors was ultimately subdued by Ximena in her expressed desire to marry him. In her role as counsellor to the king, that is, as one whose advice resolved the impasse created by the tension between her demand for justice and the king's fear of the unruly Castilians, Ximena risks her own reputation, since the justice she rightfully sought for her family has been sacrificed to her own desires. In later recreations of this episode, in the traditional ballads, in Guillén's early modern drama, and even in the movie *El Cid*, the tension between Ximena's desire to marry Rodrigo and her social responsibility to seek revenge for the death of her father are elaborately dramatized. In these later works, Ximena assumes the role of a *parrhesiastes*, harshly criticizing the king for his unwillingness to provide her with justice and in the process risking her reputation and social exclusion, a kind of death at the time.

Rodrigo's warrior skills are soon tested in the battle against three marauding Moorish rulers, including Ayllón de Burgos, whose capture brings the battle to a close (v. 530). Rodrigo takes him along with other Moorish captives and cattle to Tudela de Duero and sends word of his victory to the king at Zamora. The king responds with great joy ("¡Ay Dios, qué gran alegría fazía el rey castellano" v. 536), imagining that Rodrigo has brought the booty to him for the purpose of conveying the traditional "quinto" ["fifth part"] (v. 544) that a vassal of the king would owe his lord. The king travels from Zamora to meet Rodrigo with a royal retinue of counts and other grandees ("ricos omnes" v. 537), while Rodrigo awaits him with his vassals and Moorish captives. The encounter does not go well for the young king, likely shaming him before his high-born company. Yet the focus of the narration is not on the physical or psychological response to the shaming of the king, it rests instead on Rodrigo's statements that reflect his determination to not bend to the will of the king but to establish his independence of thought and action before the king and the witness of his own vassals and captives, all of whom are invoked in the exchange. In their encounter, the king's expectations are dashed by Rodrigo's earnest responses to his requests, and in the process, Rodrigo is seen to rise in estimation while the king descends into shameful irrelevance.

Rodrigo's introductory greeting sets the tone for the episode, as he states that he brings his captives before the king, even though he is emphatically not the king's vassal and thus has no obligation to do so. This same passage includes the poem's only other reference to Rodrigo's initiatory vow to win five pitched battles before submitting to the king, and therefore, as Rodrigo states clearly, he is not yet the king's vassal.

> "Cata," dixo, "buen rey, qué te trayo, maguera non só tu vassallo.
> De çinco lides que te prometí el día que tú me oviste desposado,
> vençido he la una, yo cataré por las quatro."   (vv. 540–2)

> "See," he said, "Good King, what I bring you, even though I'm not your vassal./Of the five battles that I promised you the day you betrothed me,/I have won the first, I will take care of the other four."

The king seems to think that Rodrigo is looking for absolution and offers to forgive him if he'll turn over a fifth of his booty. In other words, if he'll comport himself as his vassal, paying the king a fifth of the booty, the king will forgive him. But Rodrigo is not interested in the king's forgiveness. His focus is on charity to the poor ("los mesquinos"), rewarding those who have helped him in his victory ("aquellos que me aguardaron"), and in tithing to the church ("los diezmos").

> Essas oras dixo el buen rey, "Por todo seas perdonado,
> en tal que me dés el quinto de quanto aquí has ganado."
> Estonçe dixo Rodrigo, "Solamente non sea pensado,
> que yo lo daré a los mesquinos, que assaz lo han lazrado.
> Lo suyo daré a los diezmos, que non quiero su pecado.
> De lo mio daré soldadas a aquellos que me aguardaron."   (vv. 543–8)

> Then the good king said, "You will be forgiven everything,/provided you give me the fifth of all you have won here."/Then Rodrigo said, "I wouldn't even think of it,/I'll give it to the poor, for they have suffered enough./I'll give the tithers their portion, for I don't want to be in sin./ From my portion, I will pay those who protected me."

Here again Rodrigo's response is reasonable, his preference for distributing his hard-won booty to the poor, the church, and the men who actually helped him achieve victory makes perfect sense. In his reasoned response, he also dismisses the king's offer of forgiveness in return for one fifth of the booty.

The king still tries to bend Rodrigo to his will, telling him to at least hand over the Moorish captive Ayllón de Burgos ("ese moro lozano" v. 549). Rodrigo is once again compelled to deny the king's request and explain his reasoning, which is based on his sense of a nobleman's honour ("por quanto yo valgo" v. 551), according to which a noble who is taken prisoner by another noble should never be dishonoured. In addition, Rodrigo plans to give the fifth that the king hoped to have for himself to his vassals, for they have earned it ("lo han lazerado" v. 554).

> Essas oras dixo el buen rey, "Dame a esse moro lozano."
> Estonçe dixo Rodrigo, "Solamente non sea pensado,
> que non, por quanto yo valgo,
> que fidalgo a fidalgo, quandol' prende, non deve dessonrarlo.
> De más non vos daré el quinto, sinon de aver monedado,
> que darlo he a mis vassallos, que assaz me lo han lazerado."   (vv. 549–54)

Then the good king said, "Give me that brazen Moor." /Then Rodrigo said, "I wouldn't even think of it, /not at all, not for all that I am worth, /for among noblemen, when one is captured, he should not be dishonoured. /I will give you nothing more than a fifth of the coins, /I will give the rest to my vassals, who have sacrificed so much for me."

The exchange then leads to a diminished stature for the king and a heightened relevance for Rodrigo. Although the expression of the narration is brief to the point of seeming cryptic, it does state that three hundred of the king's men abandoned him and joined Rodrigo, "Despediéronse del rey e bessáronle la mano. /Trezientos cavalleros fueron por cuenta, los que allí fueron juntados" ["They left the king and kissed his (Rodrigo's) hand. /There were three hundred knights in all, those who were gathered there"] (vv. 555–6). This development confirms the strength of Rodrigo's arguments to the king. They are not rebellious in nature; he is standing up for what he considers to be right, not bowing to the pressure of rank, and in the process making a convincing case for bold leadership that many of the king's vassals find compelling. In other words, Rodrigo has spoken truth to power and in the process won over new and committed vassals. His message is one of nobles fighting independently of their kings, and of a code of conduct among nobles that need not look to the king for legitimacy.

Subsequently Rodrigo speaks with his prisoner, the Moorish king Burgos, showing him due respect and high regard. In return Rodrigo wins his loyalty and voluntary vassalage, along with the promise of yearly tribute, such that in four years Rodrigo became rich and prosperous (vv. 557–72). In sum, the king's treatment of Rodrigo, laced with a sense of arrogance and entitlement, ends in the king's own disgrace and shame, whereas Rodrigo's dealings with his captive, whom he treats with respect and gratitude, culminates with heightened status and prosperity. All of this takes place in one scene, the encounter between Rodrigo, his Moorish prisoner, and the king. The contrast is clear, although not expressed directly in the narration. The lesson learned is not one of rebellion,[12] but of the importance of showing respect, magnanimity, and fair dealing in the treatment of others, enemies and allies alike. Rodrigo is early into his passage into adulthood, but already his behaviour is far more exemplary and ennobling than that of the king.

The scenes reviewed thus far have shown Ximena and Rodrigo to be enviable models of exemplary conduct and its corollary, truth-telling. In contrast, King Fernando is portrayed as immature and indecisive, and these traits are reinforced when viewed against the behaviour of Rodrigo and Ximena. Ximena does not appear again in the poem, so her

portrayal does not evolve. Rodrigo continues to carry himself throughout the poem as a strong leader with clear values who stands tall in
contrast to the words and actions of other warriors of his social class
and to his king. Rodrigo's encounter with a leper on the pilgrim road
to Santiago is an example of this contrast; in this case his exemplary
Christian charity is displayed against the considerably less admirable
actions of his vassals.[13]

The encounter with the leper occurs as Rodrigo is returning from his
pilgrimage to the Christian shrine of Santiago, Saint James, apostle of
Christ. Rodrigo's three hundred vassals see the leper ("gapho") immobilized, unable to cross a river, and as they ride past, they spit on him
to accentuate his misfortune. Rodrigo alone takes pity on the suffering
man. Taking him by the hand, he lifts him onto his horse and transports
him under the protection and comfort of his cape (vv. 633–44). That
night in their camp, Rodrigo shares his bed with the leper. As Rodrigo
sleeps, the leper speaks to him in a dream:

> "¿Dormides, Rodrigo de Bivar? Tiempo has de ser acordado,
> mensagero só de Cristus, que non soy malato.
> Sant Lázaro só, a ti me ovo Dios enbiado,
> que te dé un resollo en las espaldas, que en calentura seas entrado,
> que quando esta calentura ovieres, que te sea menbrado,
> quantas cossas comenzares, arrematarl'ás con tu mano."
> Diol' un resollo en las espaldas, que a los pechos le ha passado,
> Rodrigo despertó e fue muy mal espantado,
> cató en derredor de sí e non pudo fallar el gapho,
> menbróle d'aquel sueño e cavalgó muy privado.   (vv. 646–55)

"Are you sleeping, Rodrigo de Vivar? It is time for you to awaken,/I am a
messenger of Christ, I am not a leper./I am Saint Lazarus, God sent me to
you,/to blow a breath of air on your back, for a fever to come over you,/
and once you sense this fever, you should remember,/that anything you
undertake, you will be able to complete it successfully."/He blew a breath
of air on his back that passed into his chest,/Rodrigo awoke and was very
badly frightened,/he looked all around and could not find the leper,/he
remembered that dream and rode off quickly.

The poem thus presents Rodrigo as charitable through his own
actions and in contrast with his vassals, three hundred high-born men
("tresçientos fijos dalgo" v. 633), all of whom curse the leper as they
ride past, while Rodrigo alone stops to offer him assistance. Additionally, the leper validates Rodrigo's charity as he reveals himself to be

Saint Lazarus, a messenger sent by Christ, who brings a message from God, that when he feels his warm breath, subsequently characterized by Guillén de Castro as the Holy Spirit (*Las mocedades del Cid* vv. 2305–7; see also Montaner, "Rodrigo y el Gafo" 126–9), Rodrigo will sense the battle fever, "furia guerrera" for Armistead ("La 'furia guerrera'" 74–7), and be assured of victory. The truth of the vision and its message is confirmed in the subsequent episode when Rodrigo defeats Martín González for the city of Calahorra after feeling the warm breath pass through him. The message from the dream vision of Saint Lazarus also fills Rodrigo with fear, but it is not crippling, most likely meant to register amazement, but certainly marking the entire episode as remarkable.

The episode in which affect plays a more prominent role and Rodrigo's advice is at its most aggressive, as well as ironic, but certainly not rebellious, involves a letter sent to King Fernando from the king of France, the (Holy Roman) German emperor, the patriarch, and the pope, demanding that Spain pay a yearly tribute to France, with detailed enumeration of that tribute (vv. 805–17). The letter is unsettling, no doubt, but Fernando's response is even more so, as he slaps himself repeatedly with the palms of both hands while lamenting his situation as a young king easily manipulated by foreign powers. Impotent, whiny, and wholly unbefitting of a king.

> Quando esto oyó el buen rey don Fernando,
> batiendo va amas las palmas, las azes quebrantando,
> "¡Pecador sin ventura!, ¿a qué tiempo só llegado?
> Quantos en España visquieron nunca se llamaron tributarios,
> a mí veenme niño e sin sesso e vanme soberviando,
> más me valdría la muerte que la vida que yo fago."   (vv. 818–23).

> When the good king don Fernando heard this,/he began slapping himself with both hands, bruising his face,/"Luckless sinner! What am I supposed to do?/No one who lived in Spain was ever called a tributary,/they see me as young and inexperienced and keep bullying me,/I'd be better off dead than living like this."

It is a pitiful sight, the image of the king of León slapping himself and lamenting his inability to stand up to these powerful foreign bullies. He sees himself as vulnerable and his response is to cry out in helpless despondency. On the one hand, it is a natural and unfiltered reaction to anger and surprise, but on the other it is an artful portrayal designed to make even more meaningful the strength of character and decisiveness of Rodrigo, who is about to arrive at the king's court. The king is clearly lost without him.

After the king's outburst, a previous episode is first resolved, in which treasonous counts were captured and now are to be pardoned at Rodrigo's insistence, presumably because they'll be needed in the upcoming fight for Spain's independence. The king's response is inflected with gratitude toward Rodrigo as he anticipates his role as the leader of the armies of Spain that will soon be marching their way to the gates of Paris, to confront the European powers that are trying to subdue him ("Françia e Alemaña … e el papa de Roma").

> "Señor, perdona aquestos condes, sin arte e sin engaño."
> "Yo los perdono, sin arte e sin engaño,
> por non te salir, Rodrigo, de mandado,
> que los çinco reys d'España quiero que anden por tu mano.
> Ca Françia e Alemaña fázenme tributario,
> e el papa de Roma, que debía vedarlo.
> Vedes aquí su previllegio, con su sello colgado."   (vv. 830–6)

> "Sire, pardon these counts, without trickery and without deceit."/
> "I pardon them, without trickery and without deceit,/so as to not disobey,
> Rodrigo, your command,/for I want the five kings of Spain to be led by
> your hand./For France and Germany want to make me a tributary,/and the
> pope of Rome, who should prohibit it./See here his decree, with his hang-
> ing seal."

The king is despondent, not knowing how to respond to the demands from abroad, and so he preemptively makes Rodrigo the head of the combined armies of Spain, desperate for Rodrigo to take charge. Rodrigo's response is decisive and inspiring and especially sharp in its contrast to the helplessness of the king.

> Estonçe dixo Rodrigo, "Por ende sea Dios loado,
> ca vos enbían pedir don, vós devedes otorgarlo.
> Aún non vos enbía pedir tributo, mas enbíavos dar algo,
> mostrarvos he yo aqueste aver ganarlo.
> Apellidat vuestros regnos, desde los puertos de Aspa fasta en Santiago,
> sobre lo suyo lo ayamos, lo nuestro esté quedado.
> Si non llego fasta París non devía ser nado."   (837–43)

> Then Rodrigo said, "Then God be praised,/for they send asking you for a
> gift, you should grant it./He is not even asking you for tribute, rather he

wants to give you riches,/I'll show you how to take this wealth./Call your kingdoms to arms, from the mountain passes of Aspe as far as Santiago,/let us take it from them, and leave ours where it is./If I don't make it to Paris I should never have been born."

Rodrigo not only accepts the challenge, he mocks the demand for tribute by ignoring it, saying that there is no demand for tribute ("non vos enbía pedir tributo"), (what) they are asking for (is) a gift ("ca vos enbían pedir don"), and his enemies want to make the king rich ("enbíavos dar algo"), while Rodrigo will show the king how to win the booty ("mostrarvos he yo aqueste aver ganarlo"). They will take the booty from the very enemies who have demanded tribute ("sobre lo suyo lo ayamos"), and in this way the tribute will come from their enemies and not from their own resources ("lo nuestro esté quedado"). He then vows to reach the very gates of Paris, or his life will not be worth living (v. 343).

The way that Rodrigo speaks to the king here is noteworthy in that his objective is to support the king, but at the same time his tone is one of encouragement and a kind of mentorship. The focus of the episode has shifted from the image of King Fernando repeatedly slapping himself with both hands in an expression of utter despondency, to Rodrigo's mocking the Europeans' demand and vowing to take the tribute from the French themselves, as a way to reinforce Spain's independence and to establish its superiority over France. This is, of course, exactly what happens, and so Rodrigo's promise is not the haughty boast that it may seem at first, it is another vow that is well within his ability to fulfill. In the process, he rescues King Fernando from his despair and sets in motion their joint triumph, the humiliation of France on French soil, into its very heart, the city of Paris. In the annals of fictional history, this campaign becomes legendary and is the justification for the king's sobriquet "par de emperador" ["equal to an emperor"].

> Por esta razón dixieron el buen don Fernando, par fue de emperador. (v. 844)
> For this reason they called him the good don Fernando, he was equal to an
>   emperor
>
> …
>
> A pessar de françesses, los puertos de Aspa passó,
> a pessar de reys e de emperadores,
> a pessar de romanos, dentro en París entró,
> con gentes honradas que de España sacó,   (vv. 855–8)

In spite of the French, he traversed the mountain pass of Aspe,/in spite of
kings and of emperors,/in spite of the Romans, he entered into Paris,/with
honourable people that he brought from Spain,

…

con ellos va Rodrigo, de todos el mejor.   (v. 874)
with them goes Rodrigo, the best of all.

This episode is not part of a progression towards fulfilment of
the vow Rodrigo pronounced at his betrothal, nor does it constitute
a verbal dispute between an authority figure and a rebel (following Funes xlix). It portrays King Fernando in a moment of "high
pathos" (following Ahern 285), as he repeatedly slaps himself with
both hands in a show of despondency and helplessness. The plotting
of the story has slowed down in order to focus on the description
of the "gestures and tremulations" of the despondent king (following Ahern 286). The king's response, he is "beside himself," and the
transformative effect it has on him, is also the conduit through which
Rodrigo's brash confidence and natural aggression are welcomed by
the king, who instinctively offers him the leadership of the armies of
Spain (v. 833) when earlier he might have been more concerned with
dictating the terms of their engagement, or with looking for ways to
benefit from Rodrigo's success. The king's affective response to the
letter and demands of the king of France has created a psychic space
that allows for a new social arrangement between Rodrigo and his
king, one that transcends the conventional relationship between lord
and vassal. The poem then makes clear that because the king and
Rodrigo have come together in this unprecedented way, they will go
on to accomplish great things, creating the legacy of King Fernando
for which he is known to the audience of the poem, as "par … de
emperador" (v. 844).

The depiction of a despondent King Fernando is surprising in the
degree of his helplessness and abject dependence on Rodrigo. If the
poem were being written for a royal audience or even one of courtiers, then the response would surely be condemnation of the king's
behaviour, a low point of despondency from which the king's reputation should never recover. In this regard, a much less emphatic infrac-
tion of the courtly expectations regarding royal conduct contributes to
a negative portrayal of Alfonso X in the chronicle of his reign written
by Fernán Sánchez de Valladolid for his patron Alfonso XI (1311–50),
the great grandson of Alfonso X. In the relevant passage, Alfonso X is

weeping over the prematurely reported sudden death of his son, San-cho IV, while one of his advisors, a courtier, follows him into his chamber to reproach him for his behaviour (Bergqvist 81). In analysing the scene and its intended meaning, Kim Bergqvist recalls that the chronicler's intent in composing his work was to contrast the "pitiful reign" of Alfonso X with the more successful rule of his great grandson (81). In this context, the king's private emotions can be understood as overwhelming the political demands placed on him, and thus distracting him from his duties. By not managing his emotions sufficiently, Alfonso comes across as a weak ruler, and the scene in question is meant to portray him in a straightforwardly negative fashion (Bergqvist 87).

Additionally, in *Castigos del rey don Sancho IV*, the narrator, presumably Sancho IV (reigned 1284–95), son of Alfonso X, reminds his own son Fernando IV, that a king must hold himself to higher standards of conduct than anyone else, since he sets the example for all others to follow: "assí el rey deue seer esmerado entre todos los omnes en buena creençia e en buenas costumbres, ca a enxemplo del rey se tornan todos los otros" ["in this way the king should exceed all men in good beliefs and in good customs, for in the example of the king all others follow'] (*Castigos* 143, cited in Bergqvist 96). Also, and perhaps more to the point of the *Mocedades* passage, Sancho IV also counsels his son, as the future king Fernando IV, to be measured in his actions, "Non cae al rey ser des-mesurado en el lugar ó debe auer mesura" ["It is not appropriate for the king to be immoderate where there should be moderation"] (*Castigos* 149, also cited in Bergqvist 91).

Additional examples of the expectation for the containment of emotions are identified by Bergqvist in the Catalan and Castilian literature of the thirteenth and fourteenth centuries, all of which are prescriptive in nature. Much more abundant in the literary texts of the period of course are depictions of behaviour, some exemplary and others inviting condemnation. Any text from the period would serve up abundant examples, as in the *Cantar de mio Cid*, in which one of the behaviours attributed to the mature Rodrigo is *mesura* ("self-restraint," or more literally "measure"). This characteristic is deftly contrasted with the king's vengeful ire in the initial verses of the poem (*Cantar* vv. 15–53), and in an especially salient example near the end of the poem, to the vulgar wantonness of Asur Gonçalez (vv. 3383–9), the elder brother of the infantes de Carrión, all enemies of the Cid.

Based on the source materials examined, Bergqvist concludes that self-restraint was an ideal projected onto the king, and as such, it was also a desirable trait in the nobility and among the knighthood (92). But this statement applies only to the context in which it was made, in a study of royal prose texts, namely chronicles of the reigns of kings, a mirror of princes meant to educate Fernando IV (*Castigos del rey Sancho IV*), and a legal treatise attributed to Alfonso X and composed in an effort to bolster his status as the ultimate arbiter of justice in his realm (*Siete partidas*). These texts were intended to bolster the image and the status of kings.[14]

Along with the *MR*, the *Cantar de mio Cid*, the *Fernán González*, and the prose versions of the story of Bernardo del Carpio in Lucas de Tuy's *Chronicon mundi*, together constitute another literary tradition in which the warrior nobility is portrayed as exemplary while their sovereigns are represented as lacking in leadership and right-thinking. In the *Mocedades* we can appreciate the hero's exemplary behaviour in his own acts, in the way his acts and his words challenge his king, and later in the poem as Rodrigo endeavours to mentor the young King Fernando by giving wise counsel and inculcating in him the character and mindset of the warrior class. This didactic quality, the mentorship of the young king by Rodrigo, is one of its unique characteristics and an outgrowth of Rodrigo's beginnings as a *parrhesiastes*, who exposed himself to danger by speaking unadorned truth first to his father, and later to his sovereign.

A few examples from the French campaign readily come to mind as helpful in establishing this conduct. The first involves the defeat and capture of the count of Savoy, who quickly offers his daughter, his lone heir, to Rodrigo as ransom for his own freedom. Rodrigo accepts the offer but then takes the young woman to his king to serve as his captive concubine. At first the king declines, saying that they have come to France to fight, not for women, and if he wanted a woman for himself, they would find plenty in Spain. In Rodrigo's response, it becomes clear that the king is missing the point. Rodrigo demands that the king take the count's daughter sexually ("Embarragand a Francia"), gently translated here as "Make France your mistress," producing a strong affective response in readers even today.

> Essas oras dixo el rey, "Sólo non sea penssado,
> ca por conquerir reinos vine acá, ca non por fijas dalgo,
> ca nós las quesiéramos, en España falláramos afartas."
> Essas oras dixo Rodrigo, "Señor, fazedlo privado.
> ¡Enbarraganad a Françia!, sí a Dios ayades pagado.
> Suya será la dessonra, irlos hemos denostando,
> assí bolveremos con ellos la lid en el campo."   (vv. 1041–7)

At that moment the king said, "Don't even think about it,/for I came here to conquer kingdoms, not for noblewomen,/for if we wanted them, in

Spain we would find plenty."/ At that moment Rodrigo said, "Sire, do it quickly./Make France your mistress!, may you please God./The dishonour will be theirs, we need to keep insulting them, /that's how we will get them back into battle on the field."

In his deflection of Rodrigo's gift, the king fails to see a strategic purpose in defiling the count's daughter. Rodrigo is thinking one step ahead and points out that it's a way to give injury to the French psyche and so compel them to safeguard their honour by re-engaging the Spanish in battle, which is his ultimate goal and strategy for victory. Otherwise, they might well decide to retreat and make it impossible for the Spanish to defeat them and plunder their riches. Rodrigo is here depicted as forward looking and is schooling the king in strategic thinking.

As a final insight into the importance of Rodrigo's role as a mentor to King Fernando, the meeting that takes place between the king and Rodrigo, on the Spanish side, and the European powers aligned against them, is instructive. Here there is no real affective confrontation, and so the encounter itself is not exceptionally memorable, although its denouement certainly is, as the daughter of the count of Savoy gives birth to a baby boy, forcing a truce in the conflict and frustrating the Spanish plan to defeat the French in battle. As Rodrigo and King Fernando approach the king of France and his European allies, Rodrigo's advisory role becomes evident:

> En seños cavallos cavalgan entre el rey e el castellano,
> amos lanças en las manos, mano por mano fablando,
> aconsejándole Ruy Díaz a guissa de buen fidalgo,
> "Señor, en aquesta fabla, sed vós bien acordado,
> ellos fablan muy manso e vós fablat muy bravo,
> ellos son muy leídos e andarvos han enganando.
> Señor, pedildes batalla para cras, en el alvor quebrando."   (vv. 1140–6)

Each on his own horse the king and the Castilian ride together,/both with lance in hand, speaking to each other,/Ruy Díaz counselling him in the manner of a good nobleman, /"Sire, in this negotiation, you must pay attention,/they speak very softly so you speak very boldly,/they are well-read and they will be trying to deceive you./Sire, request battle for tomorrow, at the crack of dawn."

The king and his prize vassal are both now performing their duties in a harmonious fashion, each one in his rightful place. The poem sees them as exemplary in their respective roles. Rodrigo has been successful in his mentorship of the king, who can now exercise his authority and fulfill his role as ruler with confidence and trust in his prize vassal, Rodrigo. As long as the trust between them persists, Rodrigo can deploy his talents as the leader of the king's armies and in this way provide support for the king and for his kingdom to thrive. Unlike the chronicle texts of other kings reviewed earlier, King Fernando is not singled out for condemnation for behaviour, but is singularly favoured and mentored by Rodrigo, whose efforts are directed to his success. In this narrative, the ideal behaviour emanates from Rodrigo and not from the king or other high nobility (recall the traitorous counts, vv. 746–89). Rodrigo then uses the status and privilege acquired through his right behaviour to lift up the fortunes of others, most notably his king.

Another, and for our purposes, final, episode in which we see the transformative power of Rodrigo on others is his portrayal as a purveyor of tough love to his nephew, Pero Mudo, who confronts Rodrigo about what he believes has been the neglect by Rodrigo of their familial bond. The episode begins when King Fernando honours Rodrigo with the request that he carry the king's banner into battle against the count of Savoy. Rodrigo politely declines, albeit somewhat sarcastically, saying that there are so many other men who deserve the honour more than he: "tanto omne rico e tanto conde e tanto poderosso fijo de algo,/a quien perteneçe seña de señor tan honrado" (vv. 921–2). He then kisses the king's hand for the first time in a sign of vassalage and requests the honour of the first blows, which the king is delighted to grant him (vv. 924–7). In declining the king's offer, Rodrigo contrasts himself with the counts and powerful grandees, reminding the king that he is still a squire, not a knight ("yo só escudero e non cavallero armado" v. 923), even though he has already served as advisor to the king and defended his life against regicidal counts, and agreed to lead the king's armies into enemy France. Not unlike his earlier vow to win five pitched battles before kissing the king's hand or consummating his marriage, here Rodrigo establishes his own conditions for proving himself to the king before accepting any honours. By taking and delivering the first blows, Rodrigo will demonstrate his battlefield prowess and so earn the privilege to carry the king's banner into battle.

As Rodrigo makes his way to the battle amid the rush of organizing his troops for combat, he decides to fashion a banner for himself. In fashioning his first ensign ("seña" v. 931), he grabs his sword and shreds a cape ("manto" v. 932) into fifteen strips. The resulting banner is so pitiful that he is ashamed to hand it to any of his vassals. Then, through the pre-battle chaos, he spots his nephew, Pero Mudo, whom he identifies as the son of his half-brother, conceived in an encounter (likely a rape) with a peasant woman ("labradora") when his father was out hunting.[15]

Here again, this time in the rush to battle, the narration pauses in order to render a shocking surprise, a family secret. Neither Rodrigo nor Pero Mudo would have been taken aback by what they already knew, so it's likely not meant for internal narrative effect, rather directed externally, to the poem's audience. Rodrigo then asserts his role as a seasoned warrior and commands his nephew to take (and defend) the newly fashioned battle banner.

> E bolvió los ojos en alto,
> vio estar un su sobrino, fijo de su hermano,
> quel' dizen Pero Mudo, a él fue llegado,
> "Ven acá, mi sobrino, fijo eres de mi hermano,
> el que fizo mi padre en una labradora quando andava cazando.
> Varón, toma esta seña, faz lo que yo te mando." (vv. 937–42)

And he looked up,/he saw a nephew of his standing there, son of his brother,/who is called Pero Mudo, he approached him,/"Come here, my nephew, you are the son of my brother, the one my father made in a peasant woman when he was out hunting./Young man, take this banner, do as I command you."

In response, the nephew first acknowledges their family ties, but then because of those ties and the familial expectations that he feels are implied, he launches into a self-pitying rebuke to Rodrigo for not paying more attention to him and his needs. Specifically, that Rodrigo has never invited him to dine, he suffers from hunger and cold, he has no blanket or cape to warm him, and his feet are cut and bleeding.

> Dixo Pero Bermudo, "Que me plaze de grado.
> Conosco que só vuestro sobrino, fijo de vuestro hermano,
> mas de que saliestes de España, non vos ovo menbrado,
> a çena nin a yantar non me oviestes conbidado,
> de fanbre e de frío só muy coitado,
> non he por cobertura sinon la del cavallo,
> por las crietas de los pies córreme sangre clara." (vv. 943–9)

Said Pero Bermudo, "It truly pleases me./I recognize that I am your nephew, son of your brother,/but since you left Spain, you haven't mentioned it,/to dine or to feast you haven't invited me,/from hunger and from cold I am suffering./I have no cover but that of my horse,/from the cuts in my feet blood flows freely."

Rodrigo, the battle-hardened warrior, then rebukes his nephew for his complaints, calling him a "traidor provado" (v. 950), essentially a traitor to the family reputation for his whining, and tells him that if he wants to get ahead "quiere sobit a buen estado," he'll need to look after himself "abidado," pay his travails no heed "atienda mal," and know well how to overcome the trials of this world "bien sepa el mundo passarlo."

> Allí dixo Rodrigo, "Calla traidor provado,
> todo omne de buen logar que quiere sobir a buen estado,
> conviene que de lo suyo sea abidado,
> que atienda mal e bien sepa el mundo passarlo."   (vv. 950–3)

> Then Rodrigo said, "Be quiet you proven traitor,/any wellborn man who wants to rise to good station,/best be able to take care of himself,/to ignore difficulties and to overcome the trials of this world."

This advice certainly may yet ring true to some of us today, and likely no less so in medieval times. Its unvarnished nature seems to define well the kind of grit and determination that propel the young Cid and will enable him and his nephew to have prosperous lives as successful warriors, which is how they are both presented as mature men in the *Cid*. Here Rodrigo is not speaking truth to power, but he is giving honest and firm advice, tough love, to his nephew, who needs to grow up quickly as he prepares to enter battle.

> Pero Mudo tan apriessa fue armado,
> reçebió la seña, a Rodrigo bessó la mano,
> e dixo, "Señor, afruenta de Dios te fago.
> Vey la seña sin arte e sin engaño,
> que en tal logar vos la pondré antes del sol çerrado,
> do nunca entró seña de moro nin de cristiano."   (vv. 954–9)

> Pero Mudo was armed very quickly,/he took the banner, he kissed Rodrigo's hand,/and said, "Sire, I'll make you a sacred pledge,/watch the banner closely,/for before sundown I'll put it in such a place,/as never before has gone any banner of Moor or Christian."

Pero accepts the banner and kisses Rodrigo's hand, in recognition of the wisdom of Rodrigo's advice and his acceptance of it. He tacitly acknowledges the offence he committed in complaining to Rodrigo about his situation and then vows to carry the banner to where none has ever gone, presumably deep into the enemy lines (vv. 957–9).

In response, Rodrigo expresses his pleasure at his nephew's acceptance of his awesome responsibility, by doing as commanded, and is now able to recognize him as kin in a much warmer way, by not mentioning the circumstances of his birth.

Allí dixo Rodrigo, "Esso es lo que yo te mando.
Agora te conosco, que eres fijo de mi hermano."   (vv. 960–1)

Then Rodrigo said, "That is what I want from you./Now I recognize you, that you are the son of my brother."

The episode may seem like nothing more than a brief interlude, a pause in the action that follows Rodrigo's charge to lead the troops into the ensuing battle against the count of Savoy. Yet, it is a reminder that Rodrigo has not yet been knighted, and since he has finally bowed to the king, kissed his hand, and requested the honour of the first blows, it provides a setting for Rodrigo to prove his valor and fighting ability before the king and the assembled grandees. It's as if his fighting career were just beginning, or beginning anew under better terms, and exemplary in every way. The appearance of his nephew at this very moment, adds another dimension to the narrative, first in the form of an affective jolt of surprise: Rodrigo has a brother who was born from a chance encounter in which his father likely forced himself on a peasant woman. Secondly, this nephew has a lot to learn about the warrior ways and the sacrifices they require, and Rodrigo shows him some tough love and in response garners the appropriate response, positive and reformed. Rodrigo, then, as he nears the end of his *mocedades*, is passing on the valuable lessons he has learned in his warrior career to a younger member of his family, a circumstance from which they will both surely benefit.

As the poem then moves forward and leads to the long-awaited encounter between Rodrigo and King Fernando with their European counterparts, it is tempting to see the process of increased collaboration between the king and Rodrigo as the main point of the narration (as in Lacarra Lanz 477). Their collaboration has risen to a new level of mutual respect and trust, and because of their united approach, their negotiating strategy is successful in securing the decisive battle they desire (vv. 1175–83). But in this reading of the poem, the encounter between Rodrigo and his nephew would be little more than a diversion. Yet, as in the case of the king's fit of despondency, the episode is another example of the narration pausing momentarily to acknowledge an exchange between two men who are about to embark on a joint venture of great import. In both cases, Rodrigo responds after witnessing a show of affective despair and brings the other party back to a place where they can overcome the demons that had them mired in suffering and self-pity. The narration needs to move forward, of course, but the pause is where we see the difference that Rodrigo makes, by bringing together in common purpose those who have been sidelined but who desperately want to be a part of something greater than themselves. The creation of these affective bonds, first between Rodrigo and King Fernando, and then between Rodrigo and Pero Mudo, result in the formation of strong allegiances that provide a way forward with a new sense of communal purpose.

Rodrigo's role as a truth-teller, a true *parrhesiastes*, a literary fantasy from whom it is possible to learn how to speak truth to power. That is his role in the *Mocedades*, and it is what distinguishes the work from its precursors, its sources of influence, prose versions, and later incarnations. In the moments when Rodrigo does speak truth to power, an affective pause is created through surprise, an expression of anger or despair, which provides the psychic space for Rodrigo's truth-telling to have a more powerful effect. His pronouncements are memorable and, coupled with the legendary deeds that generate his ascendant status, provide the narrative coherence that some readers of the poem have been unable to discern. The 345-verse narration that precedes Rodrigo's *mocedades*, including the struggles of the early Castilian forefathers, the deeds of Fernán González, and the legal wrangling by the clerics of Palencia to have their bishopric restored, all align thematically with the struggle for independence and self-determination waged by Rodrigo, first on behalf of his family, then for himself, for Castile, and finally for all of Spain. The poorly composed manuscript copy masks this narrative coherence to some extent, since some episodes lack context and so strike the reader as somewhat adrift, but Rodrigo's fearlessness in speaking truth to power is the essence of the episodes preserved, as is the struggle for his independence as well as that of his ancestors. His truth-telling clearly articulates right behaviour, as in the exchanges with his father, King Fernando, his charitable treatment of St. Lazarus on the pilgrim road, and the advice he gives to Pero Mudo. His words, echoing his determination and grit, reveal a willingness to confront allies and enemies with the truth, ultimately backed by force of arms.

The poem is centuries before Benedetto de Espinosa's (Spinoza) account of the joy that comes with the recognition that one's sense of individuality is a fiction, an incomplete account of what it is to be fully human. For Spinoza only in giving oneself up to the immanent power of the energies that can circulate among subjects and subjects, subjects and objects, even objects and objects, can the human reach its potential for self-realization (Ahern 290). This is the fundamental insight of affect theory. Rodrigo's encounters, initially as commandeered by Ximena, but subsequently with King Fernando, the Moorish king Burgos de Ayl-lón, Saint Lazarus, and finally, Pero Mudo, reflect this understanding, although probably neither the narrator nor the audience would have been capable of articulating it. No matter, the poem makes clear the exemplarity of Rodrigo in all his dealings, and the effect he has on others is initially of disbelief, but, as the poem progresses, these encounters produce lasting admiration and unyielding allegiance, and bound together in this way, the protagonists are well on their way to becoming the envy of the world.

Chronicle Prose and Rodrigo's Epic Deeds

The narrative of the youthful deeds of Rodrigo, his *mocedades*, first appear in the prose history of the kings of Castile known as the *Crónica de Castilla*, newly incorporated into a pre-existing narrative of the reign of King Fernando I. Subsequently Rodrigo's deeds are narrated in end-rhymed verse in folios 188r–201v of a manuscript shared with the same chronicle, constituting the unique manuscript copy of the *Mocedades de Rodrigo*.[1] In both cases Rodrigo is portrayed in an apocryphal relationship to King Fernando I, count of Castile and (soon after) king of León (1035, 1038–65). The final episode of the narrative involves a fantastical invasion of France fueled by the ignominious demand that Spain pay tribute to that kingdom. Even though these narratives recreate the same deeds, they strike readers as markedly different. Scholars have explained these differences in various ways, attributing them to an evolving epic narrative tradition captured verbatim at two different points of time (Armistead, "La *Crónica de Castilla*" 45–8), or to its manipulation in one version but not in the other (Catalán, *El Cid en la historia* 234).[2] What is obscured in these points of view is the fact that Rodrigo's deeds are not the sole focus of either of the texts in which they appear, but rather part of more extensive narratives with a greater purpose. This chapter will examine Rodrigo's deeds as they are narrated in divergent textual contexts in an effort to better understand the process, methodology, and purpose involved in the creation of each narration. From this scrutiny we will derive insights into the meaning wrought from Rodrigo's early deeds by the communities involved in their re-creation.

From this perspective and the insights that are forthcoming, this analysis also intends to show that attempts to discern an original text of Rodrigo's youthful deeds is a chimera, as would be the case in the other Spanish epic narratives that have more than one version, such as the deeds of Bernardo del Carpio, Fernán González, and the mature Cid.

Variant versions are not more or less genuine, closer or further from an original, but instead occasional works put into writing for timely purposes. Poets and audiences understood this and accepted it. In fact, they must have expected as much and in the process given new life to narratives that in this way exhibited a remarkably flexible concept of heroic nature through changing times, social stresses, and political realities.[3] This approach allows us to hear the narrations along with the audiences of the time, not inquiring after a ghostly original text, but open to how the narrative unfolding before us relates to its present and the values shared among audience, author, and hero. In this way, we can experience the text along with the medieval reader or listener, witnessing the hero anew and learning from him how to respond to the challenges of a new era.

Medieval Spanish historiography first emerges in Latin, of course, but when the history of Spain begins to be written in the vernacular, first Castilian and soon after Portuguese, medieval chronicles afford increasing prominence to the Cid, to the point that eventually his deeds and persona eclipse the portrayals of the kings he served. The first of these vernacular histories is Alfonso X's *Estoria de España* (begun by 1270).[4] The different historical periods included in this chronicle were redacted by groups of scholars working independently of one another, and their labor of rewrites and revisions are known as versions "versiones," not of the *Estoria* as a whole, but of specific periods in the history of Spain (Fernández Ordóñez 11).[5] Its fourth and final part, the history of the kings of Castile, was never completed by the chroniclers laboring in Alfonso's scriptorium, but was left in the form of a working draft "Borrador compilatorio de la obra" (Fernández Ordóñez 13; Campa 59–61; Pattison, "El mio Cid" 24, *From Legend to Chronicle* 3–4).[6] In the period between Alfonso's exile in Seville in 1282 and his death in the spring of 1284, a member of his royal chamber ("cámara real castellana") managed to rework the versions of the different periods as well as the remaining working draft into a completed text known to us as *Versión crítica de la Estoria de España* (Fernández Ordóñez 16). The part of this *Versión crítica* that relates the early history of Castile under the kings of León and the kings of Castile (Fruela II to Fernando III) has long been known to scholars as the *Crónica de veinte reyes* (*CVR*). This chronicle contains the first vernacular history of the reign of Fernando I, which is pertinent to this study because he is the king of Castile in both extant narrations of Rodrigo's youth. The *CVR* contains a few brief references to a young Rodrigo, but not nearly enough material to reconstruct a narrative of his youth.[7]

Soon after the completion of the Alfonsine *Versión crítica*, Sancho IV, Alfonso's usurper son who was responsible for his father's exile, commissioned the writing of an alternative history known as the *Versión amplificada* [de la *Estoria de España*], completed c. 1289 (Hijano 647).[8] This version survives only partially and is known to scholars as the third and fifth hands ["las manos tercera y quinta"] of ms. E_2 [Escorial X-i-4] (Hijano 647), as incorporated into the *Primera crónica general (PCG) [o sea Estoria de España que mandó componer Alfonso el Sabio y se continuaba bajo Sancho IV en 1289]*. For its narration of the reign of Fernando I, the *Crónica de Castilla* (CC) draws on the *Versión amplificada*, although one or more intermediary stages of re-elaboration are likely involved, possibly with the participation of the author of the *CC* (Hijano 647–51). In none of these foundational chronicles, the *Estoria de España*, the *Versión crítica* (*Crónica de veinte reyes*), or the *Versión amplificada*, is there anything resembling a narrative of Rodrigo's youthful deeds. They are known collectively as Alfonsine in that they share some general precepts on the writing of history that are thought to revert to a vision of historical writing that emanated from Alfonso X's involvement in the *Estoria de España* project, although the claim to any originality in Alfonso's vision of historical writing has been effectively debunked (Pattison, *From Legend to Chronicle* 1–2). For our purposes, however, one feature that does distinguish the *CVR* from the post-Alfonsine chronicles is the presence in the former of statements reflecting a concern for the historical accuracy of the popular sources it incorporates when these contradict or simply have no precedent in the two Latin histories that structure their project, Lucas de Tuy's *Chronicon mundi* and Rodrigo Jiménez de Rada's *Historia de rebus Hispanie* (Fradejas Lebrero 36–8; Hazbun 5).

In a strikingly bold innovation, the *Crónica de Castilla* dispenses with the editorial discretion of its Alfonsine predecessors and incorporates a full narrative of the youthful deeds of Rodrigo, the young Cid, interspersing its episodes throughout the pre-existing narration of the reign of King Fernando I.[9] Composed during the early years of the reign of Fernando IV (1295–1312), the CC was quickly translated into Galician (c. 1312) and adopted by count Pedro of Barcelos, nephew of Alfonso X, as the principle source for his Portuguese *Livro de linhagens* (1343) and more famously for his *Crónica Geral de 1344* (Lorenzo 98). The Cidian elements of the narrative in the *CC*, his early deeds and later travails and triumphs, were the exclusive focus in 1512 of the *Crónica del famoso cavallero Cid Ruy Díez Campeador* (Viña Liste 5), subsequently used as a source for early modern plays on the Cid, most famously in Guillén de Castro's *Las mocedades del Cid* (c. 1612), which in turn inspired Pierre Corneille's *Le Cid* (1636). This same 1512 chronicle later served as the most prominent primary source for Robert Southey's *Chronicle of the Cid, Rodrigo Díaz de Vivar, the Campeador* (1808), and eventually finds its narrative incorporated in the Hollywood blockbuster film *El Cid* (1962).[10] It seems likely that the esteem and popularity enjoyed by the *CC*, in comparison to Alfonso X's *Estoria de España*, and its assorted progeny stem from its narrower focus on the kings of Castile and the incorporation of the deeds of Rodrigo, the young Cid (Lindley Cintra 230–2). In other words, the willingness of the author of the *CC* to forego the Alfonsine precedent of hemming to a precept of historical truth and to embrace the narrative fiction of Rodrigo's youthful exploits led to its unprecedented popularity and longevity, and in the process transformed Rodrigo into an icon of heroic virtue.[11]

The unprecedented popularity and subsequent influence of the *CC*, and more specifically of the Rodrigo narrative that it incorporated, seem justification enough to endeavour to understand the compositional process employed by its author. We have access to the narration of Fernando's reign as the author of the *CC* knew it, prior to the incorporation of the Rodrigo narrative, through the *Versión amplificada [de la Estoria de España]* and available to us as the *Primera crónica general* (PCG). We don't know, of course, the exact content or form of the Rodrigo narrative known to the author of the *CC*. We can, nevertheless, scrutinize the narrative as it exists in the *CC* and analyse it for insights into the editorial decisions made by its author and through those decisions discern something more about the interplay between literature and history that elevated the *CC* to unprecedented popularity in the Middle Ages and cemented its legacy for centuries.

Perhaps the most striking characteristic of the incorporation of the Rodrigo narrative into the pre-existing history of the reign of Fernando I is that very little of the previous narration was altered. The chapters that narrate the reign of Fernando I in the *PCG* are found in chapters 802–13. The *CC* begins with the reign of Fernando I, and its chapters have the following correspondence to the *PCG*: 1 (802), 5 (803), 10 (804), 12 (805), 13 (806), 14–15 (807), 16 (808), 17 (809), 18 & 20 (810), 23 (811), 24–6 (812), 27–31 (813), while chapters 2–4, 6–9, 11, 19, 21–2 are new to the narration and relate the youthful deeds of Rodrigo and his relationship to King Fernando. With one exception that will be examined in detail later, the Rodrigo material in the *CC* is not integrated into the chapters that derive from the *PCG*, it is presented in separate chapters dedicated exclusively to its narration.[12]

Rodrigo is the principal actor in all the newly incorporated chapters, although in the narration of the Spanish invasion of France, chapters 21 and 22, King Fernando assumes some agency. Otherwise, the king is absent or functions as an admirer of Rodrigo's battlefield prowess. Rodrigo is portrayed as a fierce warrior, winning battles and defeating his enemies almost effortlessly. He is devoted to his mother, taking the spoils from his first battle with him as he delivers his betrothed, Ximena, to her home for safekeeping. He is also overtly devout, modelling extreme Christian charity in his encounter with a leper in a way that disgusts his vassals but delights God. He is obedient and dutiful towards his king, and his behaviour quickly garners the king's admiration. He is also presented as somewhat unconventional. When the time comes for him to choose a horse for himself, he selects a horse that others perceive to be a nag. He demonstrates his respect for the Moorish kings that he captured in battle by setting them free, treating their nobility as equal to his own. Also, whereas the prominent nobles of Castile counsel acquiescence to the pope's written demand that Spain pay tribute to France, Rodrigo is adamant that they fight to defend Spanish sovereignty and that they take that fight directly to the French. All these decisions turn out to be the right ones: His horse, Babieca, is of course a figure of admiration in the *Cantar de mio Cid*; the pardoned Moorish kings become his most loyal allies, revealing a plot by the counts of Castile to assassinate him; they pay him tribute, they honour him as their lord, and they dub him "Cid"; finally, France is defeated and humiliated by Rodrigo and his army, sues for peace, and in the process agrees to never again challenge Spanish sovereignty.

Rodrigo is driven to act by an unremitting sense of duty to his king and to a higher power, in contrast with the conventional insecurities of those around him. He serves two lords faithfully and without compromise, King Fernando and the Christian God. So, when he vows to not lie with his betrothed until he has won seven pitched battles (*CC*, "Fernando I el Magno" para. 19; chap. 4), we should interpret this as another heroic standard befiting this exceptional figure. Rodrigo relies on a coterie of allies for his success: his mother, the Virgin Mary, God, and his relatives ("parientes"), friends, and vassals, but their support is always given in response to his leadership and initiative. Everything he achieves is linked to these co-protagonists and to his own efforts. In this narration his father is absent, and Rodrigo receives no counsel from others. He gives counsel to his king, and his good counsel translates directly into the great achievements attributed to the king, earning him the epithet "Par de emperador" ["Equal to an emperor"].

Looking at the *CC* text for an understanding of what motivates Rodrigo to fight, we see that no explanation is offered for his killing of Count don Gómez, Ximena's father, just a brief, one-sentence statement that their deadly combat followed a dispute. After that, Moors raid Castile, Rodrigo defeats them and takes home to his mother an enormous booty along with the captured Moorish kings. Rodrigo soon frees his captives, who praise him for his mercy and restraint and consequently agree to pay him tribute and vow to serve him as vassals. The killing of Count don Gómez leads to a series of responses that culminate in Rodrigo's betrothal to Ximena, the count's orphaned daughter. The most important of these responses is Rodrigo's vow to win seven (not five as in the *Mocedades*) pitched battles before consummating his marriage, after which he returns to the Moorish borderlands to fight. King Fernando chooses Rodrigo as his champion to do battle for the disputed city of Calahorra. In the midst of this combat, Rodrigo explains to his enemy combatant that although they must fight the battle with their own hands, the outcome rests in God's hands alone. Then, while King Fernando was in Galicia the Moors raided the borderlands ("Extremadura"), and Christians sent word for Rodrigo to come to their aid. In response, he immediately sends for his relatives and his friends and sets out to fight the Moors. The spoils from that victory were valued at some 200,000 *maravedis*, and Rodrigo divided them evenly among his men and without greed. When the pope subsequently writes to King Fernando demanding that Spain pay tribute to the king of France, Rodrigo responds with righteous indignation saying that acquiescing to such a demand would be a tragic day for Spain and that the honour and the good that God had bestowed upon the king would all be lost. As for those who counseled appeasement, they do not seek the king's honour or that of his kingdom. The French must be defied, and he and the king will go there and deliver to them their just desserts.

From the narration of these events we may infer that Rodrigo fights in order to obtain sufficient stature to merit his marriage to Ximena, so that through success in battle he will be a fitting match for his bride, which is her expressed hope as well. He fights Moors when they raid Castile on two occasions, although these battles also result in the taking of great booty, which he distributes fairly and without greed. He fights to please his king, as when he wished to reclaim the city of Calahorra. He also fights the French to honour God's will and the sovereignty of Spain, because Spain is inhabited by those who won it by spilling their own blood, and these inhabitants should be left free to fight the enemies of the faith. God bestowed great honour on those who conquered and defended Spain, and as such, that honour must be protected. He also fought in response to a dispute with Count don Gómez, perhaps over a question of family honour, but this is left unspoken. Rodrigo's battlefield successes bring him great honour and the fear and envy of his enemies and of the Castilian high nobility, as well as the admiration of his future bride.

The portrayal of King Fernando in the chapters detailing the exploits of Rodrigo is that of an appreciative sovereign who rewards his vassal with land and great wealth in recompense for his willingness to accept marriage to Ximena Gómez. He also grants gifts and money to Rodrigo for his willingness to fight to preserve Castilian sovereignty over Calahorra, although these gifts were destined to be distributed to honour his Christian pilgrimage to Santiago. He shows his love for Rodrigo after his victory in single combat, rushing to him and dismounting from his horse to help Rodrigo remove his armor. He may be bemused at seeing Rodrigo's Muslim vassals honour him with tribute and praise, but he honours Rodrigo by declining the offer to share in the rich tribute and acknowledges and approves of the moniker for which Rodrigo is known among the Moors, "Cid." In the episode of the French invasion, the king is a secondary figure, overshadowed by Rodrigo who supplies the appropriately defiant response to the French, organizes and leads the invasion forces, prepares the way to Paris for the king, and wins all the battles with no participation by the king. Even so, the king is remembered as equal to an emperor for this invasion and its success ("Par de emperador"). The king loves and respects Rodrigo, rewards him for his success and loyalty, and exiles the counts of Castile in deference to Rodrigo, recognizing in him a guarantor of a bright future for his kingdom. Rodrigo is pleased to be an ally of the king, but this alliance is maintained at the pleasure of the king. They do not fight together, so the victories are Rodrigo's alone.

The portrayal of Fernando I in the chapters that do not include Rodrigo, in other words, the chapters received from the *PCG*, is very different. In that portrayal, the king has no prize vassal, he has very few interactions with the nobility or the highest-ranking lords of his court. They are simply identified as individuals entrusted with specific tasks that the king has decided to pursue on his own initiative, or through counsel with his wife, doña Sancha. He is a man of God, undertaking pilgrimage to Santiago before and after the siege of Coimbra. He established the church of Saint Isidore in León and built a crypt for himself and his family there. He sought the remains of Christian martyrs from Seville for his church and retrieved the body of Saint Isidore. As death approached, he stripped himself of all worldly trappings and made his peace with God.

His closest advisor seems to be his wife, a queen in her own right, doña Sancha, daughter of King Alfonso of León and sister of Bermudo, the future king of León. At their marriage, Fernando's father, King Sancho, gave the county of Castile to Fernando, including some lands that he had taken from King Alfonso. King Bermudo initially goes along with the arrangement, but once King Sancho dies, Bermudo reneges on the agreement and is killed in the ensuing battle by Fernando and his brother García, king of Navarre (*PCG* chap. 801). Fernando thus becomes king of León. Soon after, he kills his brother García, king of Navarre. This happened after García had tried to imprison him, for which he retaliated by imprisoning his brother, and then, since King García had no other recourse and was consumed by a desire for revenge over his imprisonment ("non auiendo al de fazer estonces et teniendo muy a coraçon de uengarse del rey don Fernando su hermano quell prisiera"), he waged war against his brother Fernando and was killed in battle (chap. 804). Fernando also, fatefully, divided his kingdom among his five children, most famously among his three sons, Sancho, Alfonso, and García, with disastrous results that are known to the narrator and to his audience through popular narratives, and therefore his good intentions are explained, but his reasoning is ultimately understood as faulty.

The *PCG* thus provides a fairly stern portrait of a highly religious man whose life centred on responding to challenges to his rule by killing his brother-in-law and his brother, expanding in this way his kingdom, making pilgrimage to Santiago, praying for and receiving the help of Saint James in the conquest of Coimbra, establishing churches and supporting shrines and monasteries for the furtherance of the faith, and fighting Moors throughout his life in the defence and expansion of his kingdom. In the narration of this reign in the *PCG* there is essentially no dialogue, the narrator tells us what King Fernando desires, his reasoning, and how he accomplishes his feats. Several episodes include the counsel of his wife, such as before subjecting the kingdom of Seville to destruction "a fuego et a fierro" ["by fire and sword"]: "En tod esto departieron el rey don Fernando el Magno et la reyna donna Sancha su muger, a los que ell alto desseo de todo bien et santo ayuntara en uno" ["During all this they dialogued, the King don Fernando and the Queen doña Sancha, his wife, in whom the fervent desire of all that is good and holy were joined together"] (chap. 809). In another instance, when the Moors had entered his kingdom to raid and the king felt that he was too old and weary to fight, his wife counsels him: "et couardia que era cosa que el, del dia que naciera fasta aquel en que estaua, que nunqua el sopiera que fuera, nin pereza; que non fiziesse agora por que ouiessen los omnes por que gelo retraer" ["and cowardice was something that he, from the day he was born until that very day, had never known, nor sloth, and that he not start now and give men something to fault him for"] (chap. 812). Once she had won him over, she financed the campaign against the Moors with her own riches: "Et pues que esto touo del, saco ella de su tesoro, que se ella tenie, tanto de oro et de plata et de piedras preciossas et de pannos preciados que el rey don Fernando por aquello que la reyna donna Sancha le daua pudo el rey guarnir et guisar muy abondadamientre todas sus companns et sus omnes de armas" ["And once she had this from him (his promise to wage war on the Muslim) she took from her own treasure, which she did have, so much gold and silver, and precious stones, and precious cloths that King don Fernando, because of all that she gave him, was able to supply and prepare abundantly all his company and his men of arms"] (chap. 812). Overall, these chapters give the impression that Fernando is a man who fights for the faith and for the expansion of his kingdom, sometimes at the urging of his wife, his partner in fervent faith. In the narration itself, however, there is no access to the protagonist, Fernando is a distant figure of history that we must contemplate through the high-minded prose of the author.

The one instance in which the author inserts material from the Rodrigo narrative into a pre-existing episode from the reign of Fernando I occurs in chapter 14 of the *CC*, corresponding to chapter 807 of the *PCG*. This change in narrative strategy has its impetus in a brief mention of Rodrigo in the description of the siege of Coimbra in the *PCG*, constituting the one instance in which he surfaces in the narration. Just after the siege has begun, the chronicle states that "et en este comedio fizo cauallero a Roy Diaz el Çit Campeador" ["And at this time he knighted Roy Díaz, the Cid Campeador"] (chap. 807).[13] This very brief mention in the *PCG* was apparently enough to induce the author of the *CC* to enhance the narration of Rodrigo's knighting with additional details. The knighting episode also figures in the *Mocedades*, where it takes place much later in the narration, near the end, between the two battles of the Spanish invasion of France. Additionally, and I believe unexamined previously, the author of the *CC* also brings into the episode a related scene in which Rodrigo advises the king to make pilgrimage to the shrine of Santiago, whereas in the *PCG* narration the king makes this determination alone.

To appreciate these adaptations, the relevant scenes from the *PCG*, the *CC*, and the *MR* will be reproduced below, beginning with the *PCG*:

Andados XVIII annos del regnado deste rey don Fernando ... et pues que priso estos dos castiellos, auiendo muy a coraçon de yr cercar Coymbra, fuesse primero por Sant Yague como en razon de romeria por rogar a Dios et a sant Yague quell ayudassen a complir aquello que ell auie puesto en su coraçon.... Mas la villa era tan grand et tan fuerte que el non podie con ella nin se querie dar; et sobre esto touola cercada VII annos. Et en este comedio fizo cauallero a Roy Diaz el Çit Campeador. (*PCG* chap. 807)

> Eighteen years into the reign of this King don Fernando ... and since he had captured those two castles, desiring greatly to lay siege to Coimbra, he first went to Santiago in pilgrimage to pray to God and to Saint James for their aid in accomplishing that which he had set his heart to do.... But the city was so vast and so strong that he was not able to defeat it nor would it surrender; and in this way the siege lasted seven years. And during this time, he knighted Roy Diaz, the Cid Campeador.

It is a curious passage in that in spite of the mention of Rodrigo, he has no evident role in the pilgrimage, the siege itself, or, as the narration progresses, in any of the events leading to the capture of the city. Fernando is an otherwise solitary figure in the grand scheme of history, and all his actions and subsequent accomplishments reflect on him alone.

In the *CC*, it is Rodrigo who counsels the king to make pilgrimage, and the knighting ceremony is made specific in time and related in detail:

> En el dizeocheno año del rey don Fernando que él ouo tomados estos logares, auiendo a coraçón él de auer a Coynbra, fuese para Santiago en romería, por conssejo de Rodrigo de Biuar que le dixo que le ayudaría Dios a cobrarla, et demás de tornada, que querría que lo armasse cauallero et cuidaua resçibir cauallería dentro en Coynbra. Et el rey, auiendo talante de cobrar este lugar et porque vio que lo aconssejaua bien Rodrigo, ffuesse para Santiago, e fezo su romería bien e mucho honestamente e faziendo mucho bien. Et quando llegó a Santiago, estudo en oración tres días, et desí mucho offresçiendo e tomando muy grand deuoçión que Dios le cunpliesse lo que cudiçiaua.
>
> Et con la ayuda del apóstol Santiago, guisó su hueste muy grande et vino sobre Coynbra et çercóla.
>
> (*CC*, "Fernando I el Magno" paras. 59–60; chap. 14)

> In the eighteenth year of the reign of King don Fernando, having taken those places, and desiring greatly to lay siege to Coimbra, he went to Santiago in pilgrimage, on the counsel of Rodrigo of Vivar, who told him that God would help him capture it, and that on his return he wanted to be knighted and he hoped to receive his knighthood within the walls of Coimbra. And the king, having a desire to capture this place and because he saw that Rodrigo advised him well, went to Santiago, and made a good pilgrimage, and honestly, and doing much good (charitable acts). And when he got to Santiago, he was in prayer three days, and offering up a lot and showing great devotion that God might grant him what he desired.

And with the help of Saint James, he readied his great army and he descended upon Coimbra and lay siege to it.

Once the conquest is complete and the city secured, the king is ready to acknowledge the role of Rodrigo in the victory. The brief mention of Rodrigo's knighting in the *PCG* ("et en este comedio fizo cauallero a Roy Diaz el Çit Campeador") is here greatly expanded.

Et estonces fezo el rey don Fernando cauallero a Rodrigo en la mesquita mayor de Coynbra, que pusieron nonbre Sancta María. Et fízol' cauallero d'esta guisa: çiñiéndole su espada e diole paz en la boca, mas non le dio pescoçada. Et desque Rodrigo fue cauallero, ouo ombre Ruy Díaz. Et tomó luego el espada ant'el altar estando e fezo nouezientos caualleros noueles. Et fízole el rrey mucha onrra, loándole mucho el rey por quanto bien fiziera en conqueryr a Coynbra e a los otros lugares. Et otrosí gradesçió el rey a Nuestro Señor Dios quanto bien le fiziera en su conquista.

("Fernando 1 el Magno" chap. 14, para. 68)[14]

And then King Fernando knighted Rodrigo in the main mosque of Coimbra, that they named Santa María. And he knighted him in this way: girding his sword and he gave him the kiss of peace on his mouth, but he did not tap him (with his sword). And after Rodrigo was knighted, his name became Rodrigo Diaz. And standing before the altar, he then took the sword and made nine-hundred new knights. And the king did him great honour by praising him profusely for all that he had done in the conquest of Coimbra and in the other places. And the king also thanked our Lord God for all the good He had done in its conquest.

Rodrigo is reported to have contributed mightily to the success of the conquest of Coimbra, and other places ("e a los otros lugares"). The king rewards him for his good counsel by knighting him and praising him publicly for his efforts. Rodrigo's confident exuberance imbues the episode with a dynamism that it lacked previously, especially evidenced in the bestowing of nine hundred new knighthoods and in the king's praise for him. Rodrigo comes close to eclipsing the role of the king, but the author ensures that the king and God stand just above Rodrigo in status and authority. It is a masterful display of authorial control and clear purpose, which is to add the excitement of a youthful and vital Rodrigo to a reverent homage to King Fernando, without diminishing the authority and majesty of the king.

The changes to the episode from the *PCG* include Rodrigo's counsel that the king seek God's aid in his quest to conquer Coimbra, and the subsequent knighting of Rodrigo as a reward for his actions in the battles for Coimbra and other places. The new details of the knighting ceremony bring the narration to life and elevate Rodrigo to a position nearly equivalent to the king, but not quite. In making these changes, the author of the *CC* is doing more than simply supplying details of Rodrigo's knighting to comply with his professional duty as an historian (against Catalán, *El Cid en la historia* 243). He is crafting a new scene in a dynamic and memorable way for an audience that will surely want to know more about this youthful and vital figure. These additions and the way they are incorporated reveal the hand of a talented author who respects the integrity of the material he is reworking, but whose main purpose is to enliven it with the deeds of a youthful and bold protagonist, and in so doing, create anticipation for the additional legendary material he plans to include and the ensuing portrayal of the dynamic relationship between Rodrigo and his king.

These editorial additions seem even more noteworthy when it is pointed out that there is no siege of Coimbra in the *Mocedades* text. There is an episode that combines the description of a knighting ceremony with a recommendation by Rodrigo that King Fernando make pilgrimage to Santiago, but it is the knighting of King Fernando that is described, not of Rodrigo. The description of the knighting of Rodrigo that reflects the ceremony in the *CC* occurs near the end of the *Mocedades*, after Rodrigo's first battlefield victory over the French, in this case against the count of Savoy. We cannot know, of course, if the source materials that the author of the *CC* had at hand resembled what we now read in the extant verse narrative, but if so, then the expansion of the Coimbra episode in the *CC* using materials that appear independently across several different scenes in the *Mocedades* reveals an author exceptionally adept at maximizing the resources available to him in order to create a compelling and memorable narrative for his audience.

In an exploration of that possibility, that the source materials used by the author of the *CC* were similar in sequence to the narration of those events in the *Mocedades* and that this author transposed them to the siege of Coimbra in order to elaborate on the previous testimony that Rodrigo was knighted during that event, we will advance to a review of the two corresponding scenes from the *Mocedades*. This review will give us a fuller sense of the process employed by the author of the *CC* in enhancing the Coimbra episode as it was inherited from the *PCG*.

In the *Mocedades*, Rodrigo counsels King Fernando to make pilgrimage after the counts of Castile, envious of Rodrigo's alarming success in battle and his corresponding social ascent, conspire to have him (and the king) ambushed and killed by Muslim forces.[15] When Rodrigo's loyal

Muslim ally informs him of the plot, Rodrigo first travels to Zamora to demand that King Fernando make pilgrimage to Santiago and knight himself there. Once knighted, the king can return transformed and will then merit Rodrigo's loyal service and rightly reign over his kingdom. Coincidentally, and not mentioned by Rodrigo, the king will also be free from the danger posed by the conspiring nobility (v. 769).

> El día de Santa Cruz de mayo,
>
> …
>
> Al rey se omilló e nol' bessó la mano,
> dixo, "Rey, mucho me plaze porque non só tu vassallo.
> Rey, fasta que non te armasses non devías tener reinado,
> ca non esperas palmada de moro nin de cristiano,
> mas ve velar al padrón de Santiago.
> Quando oyeres la missa, ármate con tu mano,
> e tú te çiñe la espada con tu mano,
> e tú deçiñe commo de cabo,
> e tú te sey el padrino, e tú te sey el afijado,
> e llámate cavallero del padrón de Santiago,
> e serías tú mi señor, e mandarías el tu reinado."
> Essas horas dixo el rey, en tanto fue acordado,
> "Non ha cossa, Rodrigo, que non faga por te non salir de mandado."
>
> (vv. 694, 704–15)

On Holy Cross Day in May /…He bowed before the king and did not kiss his hand,/saying, "King, it pleases me greatly that I am not your vassal./ King, until you are knighted you should not have a kingdom,/and don't expect to be dubbed by Moor or Christian,/but go to the patron of Santiago to hold vigil./When you hear Mass, arm yourself with your own hand,/ and gird your sword with your own hand,/and ungird it as is the custom,/ and you be the godfather, and you be the godson,/and call yourself knight of the patron of Santiago,/and you will be my lord, and you will rule your kingdom."/Then the king said, as he was in agreement,/"There is nothing, Rodrigo, that I would not do so as to not disobey your command."

Here Rodrigo continues to refuse to acknowledge Fernando as his sovereign, as he has done throughout the poem. Yet he encourages the king to make pilgrimage to Santiago and to knight himself, giving him instructions on how to carry out the ceremony. Only then will the king confirm his status as lord to Rodrigo and king of Spain. The king voices his willingness to do as Rodrigo commands, just as he does on other occasions. Although Rodrigo's initial response to the threat posed by the treacherous counts may seem incoherent, by advising the king to journey to Santiago, Rodrigo frees him from the danger posed by the murderous counts. It is also true that his victory over the counts, as with all others in the poem, will be Rodrigo's alone.

The changes made by the author of the *CC* to the Coimbra episode as narrated in the *PCG* include the recommendation by Rodrigo that the king make pilgrimage to Santiago and a description of the knighting of Rodrigo. The scene presented above is the only one in the *MR* that includes both the recommendation to make pilgrimage and the description of a knighting ceremony, so it seems quite possible that the author of the *CC* had this scene in mind when he determined that both elements were joined thematically and needed to remain so as they were incorporated into the *CC*. Nevertheless, the details that he provides in the description of Rodrigo's knighting are not from the scene cited above, they are reflected in another *MR* episode altogether, Spain's invasion of France. If this episode is indeed an additional source for the formulation of Rodrigo's knighting in the *CC*, then the author of the *CC* did more than simply transpose a scene from the Rodrigo narrative. He authored a new version of these events that had been part of two different episodes in the *MR* and artfully orchestrated their integration into the Coimbra episode.[16]

Rodrigo's knighting ceremony as portrayed in the *CC* finds its parallel in the *MR* after Rodrigo has won his first victory over the forces of France, led by the count of Savoy. Delighted by Rodrigo's success, Fernando then asks him how many of his men remain after defeating 1,900 of the count's men, after which he furnishes him with an additional nine hundred knights to serve him in the next battle:

> Essas oras fue el rey ledo e pagado,
> e dixo, "Rodrigo, pues en mill e noveçientos fezistes grand daño,
> de los tuyos, ¿quántos te fincaron?, sí a Dios ayas pagado."
> Allí dixo Rodrigo, "Non vos será negado.
> Llevé trezientos cavalleros e traxe quarenta e quatro."
> Quando esto oyó el rey, tomólo por la mano,
> al real de castellanos amos a dos entraron.
> El rey enbió a dos a dos los cavalleros de mando,
> fasta que apartó noveçientos que a Rodrigo bessassen la mano.
> Dixieron los noveçientos, "Por ó Dios sea loado,
> con tan onrado señor que nós bessemos la mano."
> De Rodrigo que avía nonbre, Ruy Díaz le llamaron.   (vv. 1048–59)

Then the king was happy and pleased,/and he said, "Rodrigo, so against a thousand and nine hundred you caused great destruction,/of yours, how many remain? may you please God."/Then Rodrigo said, "It will not be denied you./I took three-hundred knights and I brought back forty four."/ When the king heard this, he took him by the hand,/into the Castilian camp they both went./The king sent out by twos the knights under his command,/until he had selected nine hundred to kiss Rodrigo's hand./The nine hundred said, "Therefore, may God be praised,/with such an honourable lord, that we might kiss his hand."/He whose name was Rodrigo, they called him Ruy Díaz.

Here, as in the knighting ceremony in the *CC*, nine hundred knights are sworn to serve Rodrigo, but only here do they also express their gratitude for their good fortune in serving such an honourable lord (presumably as opposed to serving the king). This projection of Rodrigo as the lord most worthy of service is in keeping with the overall theme of the *Mocedades*. Rodrigo is exceptional in every way, and those who serve him or, in the case of the king, who join forces with him, are sure to prosper. This is what Ximena states so clearly in the *CC* when she demands Rodrigo's hand in marriage as satisfaction for the killing of her father "ca só çierta que la su fazienda ha de seer en el mayor estado de ningún omne del vuestro señorío" ["for I am certain that his estate will surely be greater than that of any man in your kingdom"] (*CC*, "Fernando I el Magno" para. 15; chap. 3).

Although the *Mocedades* passage cited above does not reenact the knighting ceremony as clearly as in the *CC*, we do learn that Rodrigo is now called Ruy Díaz, the new name signifying a change in status akin to being knighted, stated explicitly in the *CC*: "Et desque Rodrigo fue cauallero, ouo nonbre Ruy Díaz" ["And once Rodrigo was knighted, his name became Rodrigo Diaz"] (*CC*, "Fernando I el Magno" para. 68; chap. 14).[17] If this is not clear enough, in a scene previous to his knighting and to the battlefield victory over the count of Savoy, Rodrigo states several times that he has not yet been knighted: "e yo só escudero e non cavallero armado" ["And I am a squire and not a knight"] (v. 923, also v. 972).[18] Finally, in the *MR* version of the knighting scene, King Fernando selects nine hundred knights to serve Rodrigo, while in the *CC* he ceremoniously invests nine hundred new knights, which in that context suggests that they are to serve Rodrigo. In both cases, the king presides, his actions honour Rodrigo, and his authority is never challenged.

There are several reasons that the knighting scene can be seen as more coherent in the *Mocedades* than in the chronicle. The first reason is contextual; in the poem Rodrigo has just returned victorious from battle against the count of Savoy in which he lost most of his men – from an army of three hundred to forty-four (v. 1052). The king then selects nine hundred knights to replenish his army and to serve as vassals to the newly knighted Rodrigo. His vassals express their gratitude in serving such an honourable lord (vv. 1057–8), and ride off with him to battle, this time to the very gates of Paris. Subsequently, his army of nine hundred warriors is mentioned several times (vv. 1060, 1092, 1111, 1195). In the chronicle, the conferring of knighthood on Rodrigo is meant as a reward for his role in the conquest of Coimbra. But the nine hundred men who are also knighted have no role in the narration, which suggests these two elements, the knighting of Rodrigo and the designation of nine hundred knights, were also linked in the source materials. In the poem, the placement of the knighting and Rodrigo's newly acquired status near the end of the narration makes narrative sense in that Rodrigo and King Fernando are able to solidify their relationship and present a united front when it is most needed, against the European powers intent on subduing them and their kingdom. The knighting of Rodrigo at Coimbra also makes narrative sense in that Rodrigo can be subsequently portrayed as a loyal vassal to the king.

From all the evidence reviewed herein, we can assert that the author of the *CC* inherited a text that portrayed King Fernando in a conventional way, as a God-fearing warrior who was quick to respond to challenges from fellow Christian kings, namely his brother-in-law and his brother, and once challenged, fought them to the death (*PCG* chaps. 801, 804). Through the forceful counsel of his wife, he took on many pious works, he conquered Muslim Coimbra and other Portuguese towns, and subdued rebellious Moors as the need arose. It's a conventional and somewhat distant portrait, narrated in the third person. This all changes with the addition of the Rodrigo material, which includes the addition of lively dialogue, as in Ximena's plea to King Fernando to marry her to Rodrigo (*CC*, "Fernando I el Magno" para. 15; chap. 3), mentioned earlier; Rodrigo's dialogue with Saint Lazarus (paras. 28–30; chap. 7), also with don Martín González as they fight for Calahorra (paras. 34–5; chap. 8), the plea from doña Elena for an act of mercy from Rodrigo as she and Count García go into exile (para. 42; chap. 9), and finally Rodrigo's harangue on the audacity of the French in demanding tribute from Spain and the need to take the fight to them (para. 101; chap. 21). These are all exemplary moments, fit for instruction or edification, but they also enliven the story of Fernando I, by focusing some of the limelight on Rodrigo, of course, but also because they enhance Fernando's portrayal by associating him with Rodrigo and his exuberant will to succeed, his acts of Christian charity, and his lived affirmation of God's grace.

In the *Mocedades* the Rodrigo narrative projects a much different social context, probably for a very different audience. Yet here as well it is safe to say that the narrative as a whole and the portrayal of Rodrigo and his deeds within it are complementary in that they share a similar tone and celebrate heroic acts of defiance against established authority.[19] As the narrative progresses this defiance is directed more externally, against the king of France and the pope, rather than internally, as initially, against King Fernando and the Castilian high nobility, but it never disappears. In both cases, the *CC* and the *MR*, a series of exploits that comprise the youthful deeds of Rodrigo were deployed by individual authors for their own purposes within a wider narrative context, and in that process the deeds themselves were re-elaborated to better reflect the overall message that the texts were meant to convey. This process is not governed by a concern for historical accuracy, the criterion stated by the authors of the Latin and vernacular chronicles that first included popular heroic narratives, such as Lucas de Tuy, Rodrigo Jiménez de Rada, and the compilers who labored anonymously in the Alfonsine scriptorium. The authors of the *CC* and of the *MR* are more inclined to portray their protagonists with bold and clearly defined characteristics and attitudes that will resonate with their audiences and lead to their recall and celebration. In this way, Rodrigo and Fernando become literary figures who, having been freed from the truth-seeking strictures of historical prose, gain character and stature in the imagination of their audience and continue to evolve in the subsequent works that celebrate their alliance through the Middle Ages and into modern times.

From this analysis we may conclude that critical attempts to reconstruct an original narrative of the youthful deeds of Rodrigo are somewhat beside the point (against Catalán, *El Cid en la historia* 243–54). What scholars can do instead is to examine the extant versions of those deeds with an eye to reaching a better understanding of their author's "process, ideology, and methodology" (Sanders 20). In the case of the *CC* and the *MR*, Rodrigo's character, attitudes, and values conform to the context in which his deeds are recreated. In the *CC*, Rodrigo and his exploits portray a kind of partnership between a vital ascendant warrior who is nonetheless respectful of an appreciative yet sober and God-fearing King Fernando.[20] In the *MR*, Rodrigo's deeds complement a narrative of memorable examples of a proud Castilian history of defiant adherence to personal and political independence. This process of adaptation is not expected to respond to judgments of good or bad, or more or less fidelity to an original. It justifies itself through narratives that delight audiences with a sense of play between the familiar and the new, expectation and surprise, and the interplay between story and history (following Sanders 25, 142). The result is a vibrant literary tradition that spans centuries and is easily substantiated by looking to the later recreations of Rodrigo's youthful deeds, such as of the *Crónica del famoso cavallero Cid Ruy Díez Campeador* (1512), Guillén de Castro's *Mocedades del Cid* (c. 1612) or Samuel Bronstein's Hollywood epic *El Cid* (1962). In these and other examples, no one would think to equate the celebrated deeds of the young Rodrigo Díaz with historical truth or a long-lost original, since they clearly respond to a more complex narrative project in sync with the ideology of a particular society in a specific cultural moment.

Chapter Four

Holy Warriors: Rodrigo Díaz and His Celestial Champions

From their earliest manifestation in the *Crónica de Castilla*, Rodrigo's fortunes are linked to pilgrimages made to the Christian shrine at Santiago de Compostela and to the intervention of the apostle of Christ entombed there. More detail and additional saintly interventions are included in the epic poem of Rodrigo's youth, and these are significantly reformulated in the early modern play by Guillén de Castro, *Las mocedades del Cid* (c. 1612). This chapter will examine the nature of saintly interventions in the legendary deeds of the young Rodrigo to better understand their role in the trajectory of the legendary narrative, from its initial emergence in the CC to its later manifestation in the Spanish Counter-Reformation.

The earliest prose text of the Cid's exploits, an early twelfth-century Latin biography of the Rodrigo Díaz, *Historia Roderici*, makes only brief mention of him before noting his marriage to Ximena, with no trace of divine intervention anywhere in the text. The *Cantar de mio Cid*, the best-known narrative on the deeds of the mature Cid, includes a very brief dream vision in which the archangel Gabriel appears to the Cid when events seem to be conspiring against him, to assure him that God is with him: "Cavalgad, Çid, el buen Campeador,/ca nunqua en tan buen punto cavalgó varón,/mientra que visquiéredes, bien se fará lo to" ["Ride, Cid, the good Campeador,/ for never at such a fortunate moment rode any man,/as long as you live, everything will turn out well"] (vv. 407–9).

The anonymous *Historia Silensis* links the conquest of Coimbra by King Fernando I of León in 1064 to the three days of prayer he undertook at the shrine of Santiago and to Santiago's subsequent intervention in the siege, the first representation of Saint James as a warrior and, more to the point, a mounted warrior (Sicart Giménez). Although Rodrigo is not part of the narrative of the siege at this early stage, he does appear at first briefly and then more prominently in the narration of the siege in later vernacular chronicles. Among subsequent Latin texts, Lucas de Tuy and Rodrigo Jiménz de Rada recreate the narrative with the same basic plot outline as in the *Silensis*.

Among these, we can turn to Lucas de Tuy's *Chronicon mundi* since it is employed in later Castilian vernacular chronicles that incorporate Rodrigo into the siege narrative. In the words of Lucas, here translated from the Latin: "The Lord heard the pleas of King Fernando, and while he fought at Coimbra with the material blade, Saint James, apostle of Christ, fought in heaven for him." Since doubters seem to abound, additional proof of James's intervention is offered: "A Greek pilgrim had come from Jerusalem and [was] in the door of the church saying prayers and keeping vigils, and when he heard the faithful praising Saint James as a worthy warrior ("bonum militem"), he said that he was not a warrior, but a fisherman ("non fuisse militem, sed piscatorem"). This pilgrim subsequently has a vision in which Saint James appears to him and scolds him for denying that he was a knight, appearing before him with keys in his hand. A resplendent white horse is then brought before the door of the church, and as Saint James mounts the horse, he tells the pilgrim that with those keys he will open the city of Coimbra to Fernando at nine in the morning ("circa terciam diei horam"). The pilgrim reports this vision to the churchmen and city elders, and they confirm that the surrender of Coimbra happened as the pilgrim had envisioned (Tudensis 286–7).

The *Estoria de España* (c. 1284), a Castilian prose history of Spain that was written under the auspices of Alfonso X of Castile, a version of which is known as the *Primera crónica general* (*PCG*), incorporates Lucas's version of the conquest of Coimbra, but with an additional sentence identifying Rodrigo Díaz (the future Cid Campeador) as having been knighted by Fernando during the long siege at Lisbon: "Et en este comedio fizo cauallero a Roy Diaz el Çit Campeador" ["And at this time he knighted Roy Díaz the Cid Campeador"] (*PCG* 487; chap. 807). The brief appearance of the young Cid in the narration suggests an oral narrative taking shape that was already significant enough to compel him to acknowledge a role for Rodrigo in what previously had been a signature achievement of the king. Additional confirmation of an account of Rodrigo's knighting at Coimbra appears much later in the chronicle, in an episode in which the mature Cid's vassals remind King Alfonso VI, the son of King Fernando I, of his family's long-standing support for the Cid: "et uuestro padre el buen rey don Fernando, que buen siglo aya, le fizo cauallero en la hueste de Coynbra e le leuo siempre adelante" ["and your father, the good King don Fernando, may he rest in peace, knighted him [while] in the army at Coimbra and always supported him"] (*PCG* 612; chap. 936). The mention of Rodrigo in the Coimbra episode is brief, and the role of Santiago in the siege is linked exclusively to Fernando, but as the narrative of Rodrigo's deeds emerges in subsequent texts, the saint is increasingly associated with Rodrigo.

The role of Rodrigo in the siege of Coimbra finds its fullest expression in the *Crónica de Castilla*, a Castilian prose chronicle on the history of the kings of Castile written during the early years of the reign of King Fernando IV of Castile (1295–1312), as noted earlier. The importance of this chronicle in Spanish literary history is directly attributable to the incorporation of the legendary deeds of Rodrigo's youth into the pre-existing narrative of the reign of King Fernando I el Magno from the *Estoria de España*. Rodrigo's deeds are presented in new chapters that are interspersed throughout the pre-existing narrative of Fernando I. The sole exception to this compositional principle is the narration of Fernando's conquest of Muslim Coimbra, which had previously included only a brief mention of Rodrigo's knighting by Fernando.

The previous chapter presents a detailed examination of the narration of the siege of Coimbra, so here it will be noted succinctly that whereas in the pre-CC narrations King Fernando decides for himself to make pilgrimage to Santiago de Compostela to pray for help from God and from Saint James in the siege of Coimbra: "auiendo muy a coraçon de yr cercar Coymbra, fuesse primero por Sant Yague como en razon de romeria por rogar a Dios y a sant Yague quel ayudassen a complir aquello que ell auie puesto en su coraçon" (*PCG* 486–7; chap. 807), in the *CC*, he makes pilgrimage at the behest of Rodrigo: "auiendo a coraçón él de auer a Coynbra, fuese para Santiago en romería, por conssejo de Rodrigo de Biuar que le dixo que le ayudaría Dios a cobrarla" ("Fernando I el Magno" para. 59; chap. 14). The pilgrimage leads to the divine intervention that culminates with the conquest of Coimbra. Through that process Rodrigo's intervention usurps the initiative for seeking divine support for the siege and allows him to share in the glorious conquest of Coimbra, which in previous accounts had been credited solely to Fernando. This transference of heroism is voiced by Fernando himself in the high praise he gives Rodrigo at his public knighting ceremony: "Et fizo el rey mucha honrra loándole mucho el rey por quanto bien fiziera en conquerir a Coymbra e a los otros lugares" ["And the king did him great honour by praising him profusely for all that he had done in the conquest of Coimbra and in the other places"] (para. 68; chap. 14).

Rodrigo's own pilgrimage to Santiago is by far his most significant relationship with the divine. It is narrated in the *CC*, the *MR*, and some two hundred years later in the *Mocedades del Cid*, the early modern drama on the Cid's youthful deeds by Guillén de Castro, his best-known play, analysed more fully in the next chapter. Although the three versions of the episode recreate the same encounter, their treatment of it differs greatly, alerting us to differences in the reception of sources for the episode and in the considerations generated by the contexts and audiences of each work.

In the chronicle text, Rodrigo had already made a vow to make pilgrimage to Santiago when he was asked by his king to champion the cause of Castile for the disputed city of Calahorra. He asked the king's forbearance in allowing him to follow through on his vow, with the expectation that he would return in time for the scheduled combat (CC, "Fernando 1 el Magno" para. 25; chap. 7). On the way to Santiago, Rodrigo happens upon a leper who is trapped in a quagmire ("tremedal"). He orders the twenty knights accompanying him to retrieve the leper and then takes him on his horse to their lodging. He later shares his meal with the leper, to the extreme discomfort of his retinue ("que les semejaua que caýa la gaffedad de las manos en la escudiella en que comían"), who, in their disgust and anger, retreat to another room. Rodrigo, undeterred, subsequently shares his bed with the leper. During the night, while Rodrigo is sleeping, the leper blows on Rodrigo's back ("resollo"), Rodrigo feels the breath ("baffo") pass through his back and into his chest, awakens, and soon realizes that his afflicted companion has vanished. A while later, a figure dressed in white appears to him and explains that he is Saint Lazarus, no longer the leper on whom Rodrigo bestowed his charity, that his act of goodwill honours God and in recognition God has granted Rodrigo a great gift:

> Et por el buen talante que tú por el su amor feziste, otorgóte Dios vn grande don: que quando el baffo que sentiste ante te uiniere, que todas las cosas que començares en lides e en otras cosas, todas las acabarás cunplidamente, assí que la tu honrra recreçerá de día en día et serás temido e resçelado de los moros e de los christianos, et los enemigos nunca te podrán enpeeçer; et morrás muerte honrrada en tu casa e con tu honrra, ca tú nunca serás vençido, mas antes serás vençedor sienpre, ca te otorga Dios su bendición, et con tanto finca et faz sienpre bien.
>
> (CC, "Fernando I el Magno" para. 30; chap. 7)

> And for the good deed that you did for His love, God has granted you a great gift: that when the breath that you felt again comes to you, that everything you attempt in combat and in other things, in all of them you will be successful, so that your honour will grow daily and you will be

feared by Moors and Christians alike, and your enemies will never be able to diminish you, and you will die an honourable death in your house and with your honour (intact), and you will never be defeated, but you will always be the victor, since God grants you His blessing, and so be well and always do good.

Rodrigo's response to this gifted guarantee of future success, the fear and impotence of his enemies, an honourable life and death, and forever undefeated, is somewhat at odds with the blessing he has just received, almost as if Saint Lazarus had not managed to persuade him. In fact, while the message from Saint Lazarus refers to success in all his future endeavours, Rodrigo responds by praying to Jesus through the Virgin Mary to watch over his body and soul, and his endeavours, with no mention of Saint Lazarus, or Saint James, the objective of his pilgrimage.

> Et leuantósse de la cama, et rogó a Nuestra Señora santa María, Uirgen e Nuestra Abogada, que rogasse al su Fijo preçioso e bendito por él, e que lo ouiesse en guarda al cuerpo e al alma e en todos sus fechos. Et estudo en oración fasta que amanesçió.   (para. 31)

And he rose from his bed, and prayed to Our Lady Holy Mary, Virgin and Our Advocate, that she pray for him to her precious and blessed Son, and that He protect him in body and in soul and in all his endeavours. And he was in prayer until daylight came.

Rodrigo resumes his pilgrimage to Santiago, doing good deeds along the way, and then returns to King Fernando and Martín González, the Navarrese champion who awaits him. Although the ensuing combat seems like an opportune moment for Saint Lazarus to demonstrate God's support for Rodrigo, this never happens. Saint Lazarus's promise to bestow God's favour on Rodrigo by sending his breath through him never materializes in the chronicle text. This may be a simple lapse, or it may indicate that the chronicler, after including the episode in his narration, felt in some way compelled to neutralize the favour of Saint Lazarus and highlight instead the protective role of Mary, mother of God.

In the recreation of the episode in the epic text, the promise of Saint Lazarus is manifested in the subsequent contest with Martín González, which is one of the ways in which the text seems more at ease with the narrative it presents than does the chronicle. In the epic version, the encounter with the leper occurs as Rodrigo is returning from his pilgrimage to Santiago. Rodrigo's three hundred men see the leper ("gapho") immobilized, unable to cross a river, and they instinctively spit on him as they pass by. Rodrigo alone takes pity on the suffering leper, takes him by the hand, lifts him onto his horse, covers him with his cape, and then at night shares his bed with him. Soon, the leper speaks to him in his sleep,

> "¿Dormides, Rodrigo de Bivar? Tiempo has de ser acordado,
> mensagero só de Cristus, que non soy malato.
> Sant Lázaro só, a ti me ovo Dios enbiado,
> que te dé un resollo en las espaldas, que en calentura seas entrado,
> que quando esta calentura ovieres, que te sea menbrado,
> quantas cossas comenzares, arrematarl'ás con tu mano."
> Diol' un resollo en las espaldas, que a los pechos le ha passado,
> Rodrigo despertó e fue muy mal espantado,
> cató en derredor de sí e non pudo fallar el gapho,
> menbróle d'aquel sueño e cavalgó muy privado.   (vv. 641–55)

"Are you sleeping, Rodrigo de Bivar? It's time to wake up,/I'm a messenger of Christ, I am not a leper,/I am Saint Lazarus, God has sent me to you,/that I breathe on your back, so that you enter into (a state of) fever,/when you feel this fever, that you be reminded,/that anything you attempt, you will finish it with your [own] hand."/He breathed on his back, (a breath) that passed into his chest,/Rodrigo awoke and felt very frightened,/he looked all around and could not find the leper,/he remembered that dream and rode off quickly.

The promise of Saint Lazarus is realized in the very next episode when Rodrigo returns to face the champion of the king of Aragón in single combat for the disputed city of Calahorra. As Rodrigo delays his entry into combat in anticipation of the breath that is to induce a fever [or heat or fury] in him ["en calenture seas entrado"], the sensation comes to him and inspires him to take up the challenge:

> Non le venía la calentura que le avía dicho el malato,
> dixo al rey, "Señor, dadme una sopa en vino."
> Quando quisso tomar la sopa, la calentura ovo llegado,
> en logar de tomar la sopa, tomó la rienda del cavallo.   (vv. 675–9)

The fever that the leper promised was not coming,/he said to the king, "Sire, give me a wine-sop."/When he was about to take the sop, the fever came to him,/instead of taking the sop, he took the reins of his horse.

The idea of a "calentura," has been translated as a sensation of heat, a fever, but a less literal translation would be in line with what Montgomery calls "fury," *"ferg"* in Irish ("Horatius" 543), or in Armistead *"furia guerrera"* or "battle fury" ("La 'furia guerrera'" 74), in reference to the concept as first identified by George Dumézil in his study of the tripartite organization of societies of Indo-European languages, based chiefly on evidence from mythic and legendary narratives. In his study of legends related to the warrior class, Dumézil referenced a segment of the Irish saga *Táin Bó Cúailnge* dealing with the first combat of its young hero, Cú Chulainn. Armistead, in turn, was able to link Rodrigo's single combat for Calahorra with the "furia guerrera" and the pagan myth of Cú Chulainn ("La 'furia guerrera'" 75).[1]

These resonances of the *Táin* in the *MR*, specifically the promise of "calentura" as a guarantee of success provided by a holy messenger of God during Rodrigo's pilgrimage to the shrine of Santiago, appear to represent the transference of a pagan mythic narrative tradition as described by Dumézil into the realm of Christianity. Rodrigo receives a heavenly reward for charitable behaviour that has the same transformative effect as the "ferg" experienced by the pagan warriors that came before him, a furious rage that no enemy can withstand and its consequent value to society sanctioned through royal favour and acclaim. The mythic essence of this power is preserved in the *MR*, although its source has now been clearly transferred to the Christian God.

The chroniclers who preserved this episode did not follow through with the concept of divinely sanctioned warrior fury. Instead, Rodrigo attacked Martín González "con muy grand saña" ["with great fury"] as a response to taunts by the Navarrese warrior that "vos faré yo que non casedes con doña Ximena, vuestra esposa que vós mucho amades, nin tornaredes a Castilla biuo!" ["I will make sure that you do not marry doña Ximena, your betrothed whom you love very much, and that you not return alive to Castile"] (*CC*, "Fernando I el Magno" para. 34; chap. 8).[2] Rodrigo's response is reasonable, but certainly not mythic. The promise of aid by Saint Lazarus is recreated in the text, but we never see its realization. In accordance with other editorial decisions made by the anonymous chronicler, Rodrigo is portrayed here as an important vassal of the king, but subservient to him, and in no sense epic.

The episode as it manifests itself some three hundred years later in the early modern drama *Mocedades del Cid* is reminiscent of its progenitors and yet its Counter-Reformation overlay is readily apparent. The play's most transparent sources are the traditional ballads that celebrated single episodes of the oral narratives of epic poetry, and the ever-evolving written chronicles. Ballads were immensely popular at the time (Arata xxxv–xxxvi), as evidenced by a publication of the *Historia y romancero del Cid* in 1605, a collection of ninety-six ballads ("romances") celebrating episodes from the life of the Cid and organized in chronological order, some ten years before the date assigned to the writing of the play (Arata xxxii). While the *Romancero* (ballad tradition or collection) provided content for Guillén's play, the *Crónica particular* or the *Crónica ocampiana*, direct descendants of the *Crónica de Castilla*, are thought to have guided the playwright in the creation of its narrative structure (Arata xlix). Additionally, minor details from two episodes in the play reflect content found exclusively in the epic poem *Mocedades de Rodrigo*. Since it is unlikely that Guillén knew the poem, these details may have come from an unidentified chronicle text or through ballads that are now lost to us (Arata xlix–l).

In the encounter with the leper and the subsequent combat against Aragón's champion Martín González, Rodrigo is described as a "galán divino" ["a divine hero"] (v. 2188), and "un David a ese gigante" ["a David to that giant"] (v. 2418).[3] Yet in other ways the episodes are much like their medieval counterparts. Rodrigo comes across the leper during his pilgrimage to Santiago. He finds him trapped in a quagmire, as in the chronicle, and calling for help. His men spit on him and only Rodrigo is moved to assist him. In this version, Rodrigo's Christian charity is more than exemplary, it is extreme, as he not only helps the leper from the quagmire, but he also kisses his scabrous hand (v. 2207). While his men stand aside, threatening to vomit, Rodrigo shares his plate of food with the leper, an exemplary contrast with the rich man in the biblical parable in the Gospel of Luke. Rodrigo is rewarded for his behaviour while he sleeps and the leper sends his breath through him, saying, "todo el Cielo te envía/la bendición por mi mano,/y el mismo Espiritú Santo/este aliento por mi boca" ["all of Heaven sends you/its blessing through my hand,/and the Holy Spirit/this breath from my mouth"] (vv. 2305–8). Saint Lazarus advises him that in the future, when he senses "aquel vapor" ["that vapor"] (v. 2343), he should "emprende cualquier hazaña,/solicita cualquier gloria,/pues te ofrece la Victoria/el Santo Patrón de España" ["take on any deed,/attempt any glory,/since victory is offered to you/by the Patron Saint of Spain"] (vv. 2347–50). We, as the audience of the play, do not witness the subsequent combat between Rodrigo and Martín González, but Rodrigo's courage in accepting the challenge, and his victory in spite of the fact that he is a "novel caballero" ["newly knighted"] and Martín a battle-tested giant, their combat recalling David and Goliath, certainly suggests a high degree of divine intervention.

A final consideration in the analysis of this episode involves the action subsequent to Rodrigo's victory against the Navarrese combatant. Assuming that Rodrigo was graced with "aquel vapor" offered by the patron saint of Spain, and that his victory included a state of rage or "furia guerrera," in accordance with Dumézil's mythic narrative pattern (although here induced by the breath of the Holy Spirit via Saint Lazarus, with the guarantee of Santiago), he should subsequently undergo a process of reintegration into society facilitated by a "femme impudique" or, in the case of Cú Chulainn, a chorus of bare-breasted women and repeated immersions in vats of cooling water, before being safely deposited on the knee of the king (Carson 50). Following his triumph over the giant Navarrese warrior, Rodrigo returns to the king's court with his enemy's head mounted on his lance, which is reminiscent of Cú Chulainn's return to Emain Macha carrying the three severed heads of his victims on his chariot. This is followed by his claim to the promised reward, Ximena's hand in marriage, Ximena's immediate acquiescence, and the king's decision to have the bishop of Palencia perform the ceremony posthaste.

This reading of the episode is not meant to diminish the parallels with the story of David and Goliath examined by Russell Sebold, but the reformulation of the medieval narrative in Guillén's play and its link to pagan narratives as posited by Armistead and Montgomery for the epic *MR* also provide noteworthy insights into the drama. The fact that both the biblical and the mythic interpretations resonate in the same episode of the play points to a narrative tradition that is at once ancient and adaptable, traditional, and expansive.

Another matter very much related to the themes that have gone before is the question of why Saint Lazarus makes an appearance on the pilgrim road to Santiago, seemingly to test Rodrigo's Christian charity and to reward him for his response. In the narration of the siege of Coimbra, Saint James was fully capable of assisting King Fernando in his ambitious plans for the capture of Coimbra. In the case of Rodrigo and the leper, no petition was made for divine intervention, yet the intervention is promised, not based on extended prayer as with King Fernando, but as a reward for Rodrigo's charitable acts. Even more to the point is the question of why Saint Lazarus intervened in the pilgrimage of Rodrigo, who set out to honour Saint James.[4]

The figure of the leper-cum-St. Lazarus evokes most immediately the scabrous beggar described by Jesus in the parable of the rich man and Lazarus in the Gospel of Luke (16:19–31), a cautionary tale of a rich man who lived in luxury but failed in his charitable obligations, condemning him to an afterlife in the fires of Hades, while Lazarus, who suffered poverty and sickness in life, receives his eternal reward at Abraham's side. Ryan Giles sees the New Testament story of Lazarus risen from the dead as an additional referent for the figure of Lazarus in the Rodrigo narrative. In this formulation, Martha of Bethany's expressed fear that Lazarus will give off an offensive odor after four days in his tomb (John 11:39) is reminiscent of Rodrigo's expression of surprise as he reacts to the divine aroma of Saint Lazarus's breath ("¡Qué olor tan dulce y suave/dexó su divino aliento!" [*MR* vv. 103–4]) (Giles 23). In his history of the Order of St. Lazarus, David Marcombe also references both stories as possible models for the founding of the Order (3–4). In the case of Lazarus of Bethany, the connection seems to be most apparent in the apocryphal account of the resurrected Lazarus attending a banquet at the home of Simon the Leper and reporting back to the assembled company his horrific vision of hell (Marcombe 4). In modern Catholic hagiography, St. Lazarus is the beggar, covered in sores, who lay at the gate of the rich man in the Gospel of Luke.

Evoking that parable, the Hospitaller Order of Saint Lazarus founded their principal hospital at Jerusalem, to care for and protect pilgrims to the Holy Places, and especially directed their efforts towards the amelioration of the suffering of lepers (Order of Saint Lazarus 11). Marcombe cites medieval opinion in charting developments from the arrival of the first army of the Christians in 1099, with a firm date for the establishment of the Order in Jerusalem "in the 1130s on a site outside the St. Lazarus posterns" (Marcombe 7), reminding us that the Order of St. Lazarus consisted of leper brothers, healthy counterparts, and secular chaplains (8). After the fall of Jerusalem in 1187, the Order resettled in Acre.

In Acre, the proximity to the Templars within the city walls contributed to the gradual militarization of the Order. Further hastening this process was a convergence of circumstances that resulted in the compulsory entrance of leprous Templars into the Order of St. Lazarus in 1260 (Marcombe 11). Of course, a knight with leprosy remained a knight, and their lives as warriors for the faith did not end with their contraction of the disease. These Lazarite knights continued to fight the infidel, bringing to the battlefield the ideology of the cloister, believing that they were God's elect and famed for their willingness to always fight to the death, a kind of "walking dead" (Marcombe 13). For Giles, it is this context of the combination of ferocity in battle and the leprous condition of the Lazarite knights, understood as a modelling of the suffering of Christ as *quasi leprosus*, that enables the hot breath of St. Lazarus to steel Rodrigo for battle (26).

After the fall of Acre and the Islamic recovery of the Holy Land in 1291, the Order of Saint Lazarus retreated to its European headquarters at the royal castle of Boigny near Orléans, in France. This elder property was a gift from King Louis VII in 1154, to the first knights of the Order to leave the Holy Land (Order of Saint Lazarus 13; Ellul 177). The Lazarite knights established and reinforced commanderies and hospices throughout Europe (Marcombe 18–19), resuming their role as military guardians of pilgrim routes, newly dedicated to those in France leading to Puente la Reina, in Navarre, and then on to Santiago de Compostela (Ellul 40–1). From this trajectory it seems reasonable to assume a connection between the presence of Lazarite knights on the pilgrim route to Santiago and the legendary encounter between the leper-cum-St. Lazarus and Rodrigo on that same route. The resumption of their role as guardians of the pilgrim routes, in this case no longer to Jerusalem but to Santiago, by the knights of St. Lazarus after the fall of Acre in 1291, also places the context for creation of the episode very near to the date of composition of the *Crónica de Castilla* (c. 1300), when it first appeared in writing.

The episode has long challenged readers, and a review of its modern reception includes some qualified expression of incredulity, but those doubts and the responses to them are worthy of our attention since their review here can lead us to an understanding of the link between Rodrigo and the knights of St. Lazarus, and along with that, a more satisfactory explanation for the genesis of the episode. The modern reception of the episode can be traced to the most prominent medieval historian of his time, the Benedictine monk Francisco de Berganza (1663–1738), who narrates the chronicle version of the life of the Cid in the first volume of his two-volume *Antigüedades de España* (1719). In addition, the erudite friar was able to provide abundant supporting documentation from his research in the archives of San Pedro de Cardeña, the monastery where he was chief preacher ("Predicador general") and where the Cid lay entombed. Berganza's version of the episode of Rodrigo and Saint Lazarus is based on the *Crónica particular del Cid* (1512), which in turn is based on the prose chronicle referenced multiple times in this study, the *Crónica de Castilla*.[5]

Before turning his attention to the narration of the Cid's deeds, Berganza acknowledges that some of the material in medieval chronicles is fabulous, but that as with any written history, we should not disparage them because their pages include fictions. In accordance with the laws of rationalism ("Filosofía Racional"), we should not condemn entire works of history or discredit their authors based on one or two cases of fabulation (391). Also, the life of the Cid as narrated in the *Crónica particular* generally concords with its narration in Alfonso X's *Primera Crónica general*, and with many other sources found in the library of El

Escorial, an accepted form of historical substantiation even today (392). Also, Berganza muses, we should not discard the silver cup because it is tarnished, but recognizing its value, we polish it and bring back its luster. Finally, following Diodorus, "que no es buen juez el Historiador, que pretende regular, y sentenciar los sucessos antiguos por lo que aora sucede; y que quiere medir las fuerzas de los Hercules por el valor de los que aora toman las armas" ["the historian who attempts to regulate and judge ancient events by what happens now, and who tries to measure the strength of ancient Hercules by the courage of those who take up arms now, is not a good judge"] (394).

Berganza vehemently disagreed with the intellectuals of his time who disregarded the medieval histories of the Cid out of hand. His work is an attempt to review the medieval narrative of the Cid's life and to provide independent documentation to either confirm or reject its authenticity. In the episode of Rodrigo and the leper-cum-St. Lazarus, Berganza writes his own narration following closely but not verbatim the *Crónica particular*. At the conclusion of the episode, he admits that Rodrigo's exemplary Christian charity may seem incredible, but then proceeds to rationalize, "Pero yo entiendo, que el lance es despique de la inhumanidad, que el Rico Avariento vsó con el pobre Lazaro, negandole las migajas, que se desperdiciaban en su opipara mesa" ["But I understand that the episode is (a form of) recrimination for the inhumanity that the miserly rich man showed towards poor Lazarus, refusing him the crumbs that fell from his sumptuous table"] (406–7). Berganza then proceeds to reprimand those for whom the kind of compassion that Rodrigo bestows on Lazarus is not believable, not so much as an historical event, but as a judgment on the human capacity for charity.

Robert Southey, in his English version of the life of the Cid, *Chronicle of the Cid* (1808), relies heavily on the work of Berganza, quoting him frequently in his notes as a guide to his understanding of the Cid's life and to the relative importance and veracity of the sources Southey employs. For the episode in question, Berganza's moralistic reasoning evidently captured the attention of Southey, as expressed in the footnoted commentary that accompanies his translation of the episode. It's an interesting cross-cultural perspective, betraying Southey's protestant bias and skepticism in his introduction and translation of Berganza's commentary:

> Berganza displays some right Catholic logic upon this subject. We believe, he says, the cruelty of Dives towards Lazarus in refusing him the crumbs which fell from his table; why then should we not believe that the human heart is capable of an equal degree of charity? And as if to show there was

nothing extraordinary in the miracle, he relates three such, one of which happened "about, if not at the very same time, to Pope Leo IX." The devotion of the Cid to St. Lazarus is brought forward in proof of the truth of the story. He gave certain houses in Palencia to form a parish and hospital under his invocation, and established a brotherhood (*Cofradia*) of knights in the hospital to attend to the lepers. This institution was revived by don Alonzo Martinez de Olivera, one of his descendants, as appears by his will, and by a privilege of Fernando IV, granted in 1296. Another proof is, that the promise of perpetual success made by the Saint was accomplished.

(10)

Berganza is a bit more skeptical regarding Martínez de Olivera's genealogical link to the Cid than what we might infer from Southey's translation ("one of his descendants"), saying instead, "preciandose de tener sangre del Cid en sus venas" ["claiming to have the Cid's blood in his veins"] (407). Although Berganza does not reproduce either Martínez de Olivera's will or Fernando IV's privilege attesting to the latter's consanguinity with the Cid, Deyermond includes a relevant excerpt from the will in his study, emphasizing that the principal points of interest (for his study) are Martínez de Olivera's claim of descent from the Cid and the reference to the Cid's foundation of San Lázaro (111).[6]

For present purposes, the question of the testator's genetic link to the Cid is less relevant than his characterization of the properties he inherited as a descendant of the Cid, and the connection between those properties and the Order of Saint Lazarus. It is also relevant to the present study to point out that the will identifies the testator as "Comendador Mayor de tierra de Leon, de la Orden de la Caualleria de Santiago, fijo de Don Martin Alfonso, Conde de Barcelos, y fijo de la Condesa Doña Elvira Sarmiento" ["Commander of the land of León, of the Order of the Knights of Santiago, son of Don Martín Alfonso, count of Barcelos, and son of the Countess Doña Elvira Sarmiento"], and its dating of Friday, 25 May 1302 (Fernández del Pulgar 378–9 [374–7 are repeated after the initial pages 378–9, so that Berganza's copy of the will and his commentary include pages 378–9, 374–7, 378–9; the pages cited are the first and last pages of the entry]).

Iten mando que la mi casa, y Orden, y Hospital de San Lazaro de esta ciudad, lo qual mandó facer el Cid, quando mandó hazer la Iglesia de San Lazaro, el qual suelo de la dicha Casa, yo huve, y heredé por herencia con los mis Lugares y todos los otros bienes raizes en Castilla, que fueron de Don Juan Rodriguez, hijo de Diego Rodriguez, hijo de el Cid, el qual murió en la batalla, que huvo el Rey Don Alonso con el Rey Moro de Consuegra, el qual Don Juan fue padre de mi abuela, D. Sancha Rodriguez, muger de Don Garcia Fernandez mi abuelo.

Iten mando, que por quanto fize la dicha Casa, y Orden, en el suelo, que yo assi heredé, y fize las casas de ella, y la cerqué, y lo mandé dar todas las cosas, que fueran menester para los lacerados que en ella viuen, y para los habitants de ella, y la doté, y le di las tierras, heras, y viñas, que la dicha Casa en esta Ciudad tiene … y fize por el servicio de Dios, y porque en los dichos pobres le cumplan las siete obras de misericordia, y piedad, y por cumplir lo que el Cid mandó hazer en dicho suelo, y por la deuocion que el tuuo a San Lazaro; mando que en la dicha Casa, y Orden no esten sino los lacerados de San Lazaro, y los que para ellos pidieren limosnas para mantenimiento de dichos pobres.

Iten mando, que la Casa y Orden de San Lazaro, sea señor de ella mi hijo mayor Martin Alonso, y la tenga con mi mayorazgo.

(Fernández del Pulgar 377–8)

Item: I order that my Residence, and Order, and Hospital of Saint Lazarus of this city, which the Cid ordered built, when he ordered built the Church of Saint Lazarus, the site of said Residence, I acquired, and inherited through inheritance along with my places and all the other properties in Castile, that belonged to Don Juan Rodriguez, son of Diego Rodriguez, son of the Cid, the one who died in the battle, that King Don Alonso had with the Moorish king of Consuegra, which said Don Juan was the father of my grandmother, D. Sancha Rodriguez, wife of Don García Fernandez my grandfather.

Item. I order that since I built said Residence, and the Order, on the site, that I thus inherited, and I built its other buildings, and I enclosed it, and I ordered it supplied with all the things necessary for the lepers who live within it, and for its inhabitants, and I endowed it, and I gave it the lands, the crops, and the vineyards, that said Residence has in this city … and I did it as a service to God, and so that through the said afflicted would be satisfied the seven acts of mercy, and piety, and to comply with what the Cid ordered built on said site, and for the devotion that he showed to Saint Lazarus; I order that in said Residence, and Order live only the lepers of Saint Lazarus, and those who ask for alms for the maintenance of said afflicted.

Item. I order that the residence and Order of Saint Lazarus, that my eldest son, Martin Alonso, be its lord, and that he have it along with my estate.

The connection between the Cid and St. Lazarus is twofold. In his lifetime he expressed a devotion to the saint and willed that on the property he owned in Palencia and on which he had built the Church of St. Lazarus, the same property inherited by don Alonso Martínez de Olivera, there be constructed a hospital (or residence) dedicated to Saint Lazarus. The residence (or house) was later constructed by don Alonso, and the Order established, along with a grant of lands, crops, and vineyards sufficient to supply them. He then restricted the house and the Order to those afflicted with leprosy, as was customary in the Order of Saint Lazarus, from the time of their early history in the Holy Land.

The date of the will (Friday, 25 May 1302) is very close to what we believe to be the date of composition of the *Crónica de Castilla* (for Rochwert-Zuili, between 1300 and 1301 [para. 30]). It seems fairly well established that in the lifetime of don Alonso and prior to the composition of the first written version of the young Cid's deeds, it was believed that the Cid had owned property in Palencia, had constructed a church dedicated to St. Lazarus, and had expressed a desire for the construction of a hospital (residence) dedicated to the care of pilgrims and lepers on that property. Deyermond reviews documentation on a number of leper hospitals in Europe and more specifically in Spain prior to the fourteenth century, but he finds none connected to the Order of Saint Lazarus (111–12), which leads him, in his final assessment, to suggest that "the legends of the Cid's encounter with a leper may have given rise to the story of the early lazar-house, rather than *vice-versa*" (112–13). Deyermond's concerns are with origins, but for the purposes of this study, the question of which came first is somewhat beside the point. The presence of the knights of Saint Lazarus on the pilgrim road to Santiago sometime after their exodus from the Holy Land in 1291, the mature Cid's legendary dream vision of the archangel Gabriel (*Cantar* vv. 404–12), and his renown as a patron of lepers early enough in the lifetime of don Alonso Martínez de Olivera to have inspired him to carry out the construction and provisioning of the leprosarium documented in his will of 1302, surely provide ample stimuli for the genesis of Rodrigo's legendary encounter with Saint Lazarus in the final decade of the thirteenth century, whether on the road to Santiago, as in the chronicle, or on his return from pilgrimage, as in the poem, in the region of Palencia.[7]

Identifying this brief and very specific time frame for the genesis of Rodrigo's encounter with St. Lazarus does not of course establish a date for the emergence of the full narrative. Legendary figures from the twelfth and thirteenth centuries are discernible in the portrayal of Rodrigo in both chronicle and poem. Bernardo del Carpio, Fierabras, and more distant in time and space, Cú Chulainn, the boy-hero of the Irish epic narrative *Táin Bó Cúalinge*, are revived in Rodrigo's deeds, speech, attitudes, and perhaps most of all, his will to fight. This hybridity may well be at the root of what some critical readers of the narrative have seen as the incongruity of the religiosity of Rodrigo's encounter with the leper. Although the word is charged with negativity, and hybridity may be more neutral, the critical observations on the episode's incongruity can serve here to reassess its ancient roots and a previous manifestation more congruent with the poem as a whole and with Rodrigo's depiction in poem and chronicle.

Deyermond notes the singularity of Rodrigo's encounter with the leper with the observation that "the charity of Rodrigo's action is in marked contrast to his behaviour in most of the poem, but the contrast is even more marked if we recall the fear and horror with which leprosy was viewed in the Middle Ages" (113). This leads him to conclude, "Thus Rodrigo's legendary action puts him in a tradition of heroic virtue and carries implications of sanctity which are curious in the context of the real Rodrigo's life, and utterly incongruous in the context of the *MR*" (114). Montaner also notes the incongruity of the episode within its narrative context, but for structural reasons. He points out that in both versions of the narrative, the prose chronicle and the epic poem, Rodrigo agrees to the combat for Calahorra but then abruptly states that he must first make pilgrimage to Santiago. This gives rise to the encounter with the leper, on the way to Santiago in the chronicle, or on his return from Santiago in the poem. For Montaner, the pilgrimage to Santiago is superfluous, since argumentatively it would make more sense for Rodrigo to accept the challenge for Calahorra and to travel directly there, encountering the leper on his way to fight the champion of the king of Aragón. From this perspective, Rodrigo's multiple acts of charity towards the leper seem redundant, since for the purpose of a divine reward, pulling the leper from his entrapment in the quagmire would have been sufficient (Montaner, "Rodrigo y el gafo" 123).[8]

The episode is more consequential in the *MR* than in the chronicle, since in the poem the breath of St. Lazarus does embolden Rodrigo in his singular combat for Calahorra, and the two versions differ in other details as well (Deyermond 113, and additionally Montaner, "Rodrigo y el gafo" 137). These differences have reinforced the theory that both chronicle and poem draw their material from another source, an earlier **Gesta [de las Mocedades de Rodrigo]*.[9] Funes identifies the elements of the extant *MR* that he considers derived from the earlier *Gesta* and dates its creation to the last five years of the thirteenth century (xxxviii–xxxix), the same period identified here for the introduction of St. Lazarus into the narrative. But if we examine the episode with its endpoint in mind, the single combat for Calahorra, then we can begin to understand the episode in an evolutionary sense, in tandem with the incorporation of other ancient deeds of note that are continually reformulated to reflect the exigencies of new social realities and concerns.

The Latin panegyric poem celebrating the feats of the Cid, the *Carmen Campidoctoris*, thought to have been composed in the Cid's lifetime (Gil 101), identifies the defeat of a Navarrese warrior while an adolescent as his first single combat: "Hoc fuit primum singular bellum,/Cum adolescens deuicit Nauarrum" (vv. 25–6).[10] In the brief review of the early deeds of Rodrigo in the *Historia Roderici*, a Latin biography of the Castilian warrior likely composed by a contemporary of the Cid after his death (Falque Rey 20; Barton and Fletcher 101), what is likely the same storied combat is briefly mentioned, this time naming his foe: "Postea namque pugnauit cum Eximio Garcez uno de melioribus Pampilone et deuicit eum" (49; chap. 5, lines 14–15). This single combat from which the adolescent Rodrigo emerged victorious is reasonably assumed to be based on an actual event in the young Cid's life. Its reenactment in the combat with Martín González ("Martin Gonzales" *CC*, "Fernando I el Magno" para. 24; chap. 6; "Martín Gonçález de Navarra" *MR* v. 573), some two hundred years later suggests that the episode served as an early nexus for the narrative of Rodrigo's youth. It is also the episode on which Montgomery and Armistead base parallels with Cú Chulainn, and over the course of its two-hundred-year progression it must have acquired and shed myriad characteristics and associations, including the transformation of a pagan "furia guerrera" into a saintly breath delivered on the pilgrim road to Santiago in or near 1291.[11]

To better understand this process of transformation and in doing so to formulate an idea of the nature of an earlier manifestation of divine support for Rodrigo, we can easily imagine a version of the visitation prior to 1291, in which Rodrigo not only sets out on pilgrimage to Santiago, but also is rewarded by the saint for his legendary will to fight. This putative episode would make the pilgrimage to Santiago more coherent, as the pilgrimage and visitation would serve the same end. After all, Saint James is Santiago Matamoros, although once an apostle of Christ (for the mistaken Greek pilgrim in the *CC*, a fisherman), by the time of the *Historia Silensis*, he is a heavenly warrior on a white horse who aids Christians against the Muslim foe. In this earlier version of the episode, Rodrigo would not yet exhibit the extreme Christian charity toward the pitiful leper and its attendant association with Saint Lazarus, thus eliminating any incongruency with other characteristics in his portrayal. This putative early version of the story would nullify the concern expressed by Deyermond regarding the incongruity of Rodrigo's charitable acts within the context of a narrative that celebrates an uncompromisingly fierce warrior.[12] The pilgrimage to Santiago retains its centrality in the narrative, so Montaner's concern about plot efficiency would not yet be relevant.

This chapter has examined the celestial champions who lend their support to Rodrigo. The encounter between Rodrigo and the leper-cum-Saint Lazarus produced a sense of incongruency in the narrative. This recognition led to the reconstruction of a hypothetical earlier stage of the episode that is more in consonance with the portrayal of Rodrigo as a warrior, relegating the attribution of a severe Christian ethos to the young Rodrigo to a later development in the evolution of the episode. The advent of the knights of Saint Lazarus as custodians of the pilgrim route to Santiago soon after 1291, and the precise dating of the first written manifestation of the Rodrigo narrative, the chronicle version of 1300–1, allow us to fix this final transformation in exceptionally precise terms. These findings in turn illustrate the capacity of oral narratives to incorporate new elements and shed old ones in the pursuit of renewed meaning and purpose for their audiences. As the narrative of the young Cid finds its way to the early modern period, its capacity to transform itself and to appeal to ever broader audiences becomes its most compelling feature. As we will see in the final chapter of this study, the Saint Lazarus episode eventually becomes fully integrated into the narrative along with a corresponding transformation of Rodrigo from warrior hero to "galán divino" (Sebold).

Chapter Five

Guillén de Castro's *Mocedades del Cid* and the Traditional Ballad

Las mocedades del Cid (*MC*) is a drama written by Guillén de Castro sometime between 1612 and 1615 (Arata xxxii). It incorporates verses from select Spanish ballads that celebrate the exploits and travails of Rodrigo Díaz, the young Cid, and follows a plot line familiar to the playwright and his audiences through chapbooks, chronicle narratives, and a ballad collection on the life of the Cid organized chronologically. Publication of these ballads date from the mid-sixteenth century, but they were known even more widely through an oral tradition that celebrated legendary deeds from an earlier time ("una especie de inconsciente colectivo jungiano" ["a kind of Jungian collective unconsciousness"] Egido, "Mito" 504). The merit of Guillén's play, its popularity, and its subsequent influence on later literary recreations of the young Cid's life is in part explained by the author's ability to transfer to the stage key moments of this legendary youth that had previously taken shape as epic verse, chronicle prose, and ballad. Along with the new dramatic format, Guillén garnered recognition for his artistry in transforming the protagonist of his play from the willful and independent-minded hero of the medieval epic and subsequent ballad tradition, into a circumspect and self-sacrificing paragon of Counter-Reformation virtue (Arata lii; Sebold 235).

The play and the portrayal of its principal characters are in accord with the cultural currents of the time, as preachers, sacred texts, and human authors promoted the virtues of self-restraint in the intellectual realm (to avoid the sin of Protestant self-examination), and in the personal (to avoid the sin of pride) (Sebold 235).[1] Guillén himself would have internalized these virtues as an aspiring playwright in Counter-Reformation Spain, leading him to portray Rodrigo as a "David (slayer of Goliath) español o galán divino" ["Spanish David or divine hero"] (Sebold 234–5). In Guillén's play, this newly fashioned protagonist is heroic in his resolve to sublimate his personal desires to the social norms of his time (Crapotta and Welles 7), a very different profile from the willful and self-assured force of nature championed in the medieval epic and subsequent ballads.

Previous studies have examined the presence and role of legendary ballads in the dialogue and the dramatic structure of the play, as well as in the expansion and the enhanced articulation of Rodrigo's role as a Christian warrior guided and encouraged by scripture and by Saint Lazarus in the role of God's messenger. In these studies, the identification of the ballads that Guillén incorporated into his play is the point of departure for their analyis (as in Arata xlvi). Yet, another and equally important aspect of Guillén's creative process is the identification of the ballads that he chose to exclude from his play, a choice between the medieval characterization of Rodrigo retained by some ballads and his more circumspect character traits reflected in others.[2] An awareness of the process of ballad selection employed by Guillén for his portrayal of Ximena, Rodrigo's sometimes antagonist and future wife, is even more critical to a full appreciation of the dramatic and didactic purposes of the play. The analysis to follow will explore Guillén's selection and use of ballads in the portrayals of both protagonists, but it is in the portrayal of Ximena that we will be able to more fully appreciate and articulate Guillén's artistry and messaging. Additionally, because the characterizations of Rodrigo and Ximena have their origins in medieval legends, they hold resonances that Guillén may not have actively sought. In these cases, an exploration of these medieval roots of select scenes in the play will serve to broaden our understanding of their affective potential for the audience of the time and for us today.

In the ballad tradition, the most affective moments of legendary characters continued to be recreated and to evolve, whether originating from medieval epic poetry, the prose chronicles that reformulated their poetic sources for a royal or clerical reception, or novel compositions that eased the medieval tropes and characters into new roles as society transitioned from a warrior culture of clan rivalries to a society governed by "razón de estado" ["realpolitik"] (Arata lxv). Previous plays had dramatized ballads on the Cid, such as Juan de la Cueva's *La muerte del rey don Sancho y reto de Zamora* in 1579 (Sebold 217), an anonymous *Las hazañas del Cid* in 1603, as well as an early play on the exploits of the young Cid, *La segunda parte de los hechos del Cid* (c. 1575–80). Although different in subject matter, these precursors to Guillén share a common technique in joining together well-known episodes from the ballad tradition without any kind of transition, relying on a common set of protagonists for their coherence. Another technique common in the dramatization of ballad material, also employed by Guillén in his plays prior to *MC*, consisted in centring the play on one well-known ballad and expanding on its various motifs, creating in this way a plot that would encompass them and produce a resolution that accorded with the tragicomic tenets in vogue at the time (Arata xlv). In *MC*, Guillén revises his approach to the ballad material, no doubt in part inspired by Juan de Escobar's chronological ordering of ninety-six ballads celebrating the Cid's legendary exploits that had been published in 1605 (*Historia y romancero del Cid*).[3] Instead of expanding on just one ballad as the creative impetus for a play, or of linking exploits from a series of ballads, Guillén chose some twelve ballads depicting Rodrigo's youth and reformulated their themes and expression into a plot based on the ordering of the ballads in Escobar's collection and on two prose chronicles on the life of the Cid.[4]

There are no accounts of the performance of Guillén's play, either in Valencia or subsequently, after his move to Madrid. Guillén published *MC* (originally a diptych with *Las hazañas del Cid* or *Las mocedades del Cid-Comedia segunda*, to be performed a day later) in 1618 as part of a volume that contained what he considered his twelve best dramatic works, just months before he departed Valencia for Madrid in search of better fortune at the festive court of King Felipe III, under the protection of the Marqués de Peñafiel (Ramos 171). The play most likely followed the conventional run of early modern dramas: a prominent theatre company would perform the play in capital cities during a season before its relegation to a second-tier company that would then embark on a circuit of smaller cities and towns until the play was eventually consigned to oblivion. Guillén's play avoided this final destiny because in the early months of 1637, Pierre Corneille, a young French dramatist, presented his adaptation of Guillén's play, *Le Cid*, in the Théâtre du Marais in Paris, thrilling his audiences and inaugurating a prolonged period of Gallic critique known as *Le querelle du Cid* ("The quarrel of the Cid"). The *querelle* involved accusations of plagiarism against Corneille, accusations of impropriety in the depiction of Ximena (meeting alone with the killer of her father was considered immoral), and perhaps most importantly to the French classicists, the breaking of several of the neo-Aristotelian dramatic precepts, including unity of place and verisimilitude – Ximena's wish to marry her father's killer was considered improbable. Literary luminaries throughout the eighteenth and nineteenth centuries continued to express their opinions on the relative merits of the two works.[5] In the latter years of the nineteenth century Spanish literary critics managed to refocus attention on *MC* from a perspective that rescued the work from the death grip of the ongoing

Hispano–Gallic polemic. Miguel de Unamuno identified traits in the young Cid that he considered *castizo*, a term he employed to designate the essence that was unique and compelling about Spanish civilization (mostly Castilian). Ramón Menéndez Pidal, surely the most influential Spanish literary scholar of the twentieth century, included a careful analysis of the play in his *La epopeya castellana a través de la literatura española* (1910), seeing it as the culmination of a centuries-long evolution of the Cid legend, thus liberating the play from its assigned role as a precursor to a highly successful foreign work of genius. In Spanish literary studies today, and in this chapter specifically, the play continues to be studied in the context of the literary traditions that generated interest in its subject and provided its content.[6]

Within the cultural context of Counter-Reformation Spain and as part of the landed gentry of his time ("terrateniente" ["landowner"] [Montaner, *Política* 86]; "familia hidalga" ["noble famly"] [Arata xxxi]), Guillén was most likely horrified by the strident rebelliousness and anger-fueled aggression attributed to Rodrigo in some of the ballad material that he kept on his writing desk.[7] In the remaking of the young hero, Guillén ensured that the balladic echoes of the clannish young Cid, openly hostile to his king, would not be reflected in the portrayal of his protagonist. Later works, such as Corneille's *Le Cid*, Southey's *Chronicle of the Cid*, and Hollywood's *El Cid* make no mention of the popular legendary hero who for much of his prodigious youth refused to swear fealty to the king or to consummate the marriage that the king compelled him to accept. These memorable characteristics were excluded knowingly from the portrayal of the hero, as part of a conscious decision to imagine a conflicted yet blameless hero whose blood coursed through the veins of the monarchy (Arata lix), and as Guillén believed, through his own (Matulka 54).

Scholars have identified the balladic sources at Guillén's disposal and the specific ballads incorporated into his drama (Cazal 121; Arata xlvi), and have documented their wide popularity and influence on Guillén's work (Arata xxxv–xxxvi). The understanding of the role of specific ballads in the genesis of the play varies somewhat among critics, from assertions of their essential importance, as in Menéndez Pidal's description of the play as a "romancero dramatizado" ["dramatized ballads"] (cited in Egido, "Mito" 506) or "Romancero del Cid puesto en acción" ["Cidian ballads put into action"] (cited in Arata lxvii), to ballad counts that have become more sharply focused over time, starting at twenty-nine (Faliu-Lacourt 163) to twelve (Arata xlvi), to a more rigorously defined five (Cazal 95, 121). The degree to which the playwright incorporated the expression of the ballads into the play has also been examined, more or less wholesale, as in the affirmation by Arata that "los romances quedan incrustados en la obra, con mínimas variantes" ["the ballads are embedded in the text, with minimal changes"] (lxvii), or to different degrees, with five being incorporated more fully than others (in this case, the remaining seven), much less so or even not at all, along with the potential for other sources, written and oral, to have preempted the identifiable ballads (Cazal 95–6).

The identification of the five ballads that were substantially incorporated into Guillén's play along with an additional seven (twelve in all) that are present to varying degrees in the play (Arata xlvi), the degree to which Guillén incorporated individual ballads into his play (Cazal), and his methods and artistry in doing so (Arata xlv–xlix), have provided important insights into the play and Guillén's creative process. Yet, Guillén's young hero bears little resemblance to the protagonist of much of the ballad tradition and thus these compositional components tell only part of the story of Guillén's reformulation of his young protagonist. An important component of Rodrigo's transformation is Guillén's portrayal of him as a "galán divino" ["divine hero"] and as David slaying Goliath (Ximena's father, el Conde Lozano), and the expansion and contemporizing of the traditional episode of Rodrigo's encounter with a leper who, as a reward for the Christian charity Rodrigo bestows on him, reveals himself to be Saint Lazarus and grants Rodrigo God's promise of success in his future endeavours (Sebold 236–41). Additionally, and perhaps more importantly, Guillén suppresses the ballads that portray the more provocative and affective characterization of the legendary Rodrigo (Sebold 235; Cazal 97).

The critical attention to the ballads employed by Guillén, and to the Counter-Reformation themes included in the portrayal of Rodrigo, leaves unexamined the details of Guillén's displacement of the legendary Cid, the hero of the medieval epic and the ballads that drew from that narrative tradition. Even more importantly, the focus on the reformulation of Rodrigo's character ignores the more compelling portrayal of Ximena, Rodrigo's co-protagonist and future wife. The ballads that Guillén incorporates into his portrayal of Ximena retain her medieval characterization as a noblewoman confident in her ability to secure justice for herself, while those deployed in the portrayal of Rodrigo reflect a later emphasis on his courtly education with little to remind us of the warrior exploits that brought him fame (Arata xlviii). In the same way that Guillén had access to ballads celebrating the bold Rodrigo of medieval legend, he also had access to ballads that portray Ximena as more reasoned and respectful of authority than her portrayal in the play but chose not to incorporate them. In other words, the ballads Guillén chose

for his portrayal of Rodrigo reinforce the Counter-Reformation culture
of his time, while the ballads he chose for Ximena's portrayal are deeply
resonant of medieval myth and mores.

The traits of the legendary Rodrigo and Ximena that inspired Guillén
to write his play and that surely drew audiences to its performance have
their origin in the oral narrative that first emerged in the prose *Crónica de
Castilla*. The prose text re-emerges in later chronicles that expand on the
narration of the *CC*, but most critically the oral narrative tradition that
predates it continued to evolve and inspired scores of ballads that recreate, imagine, or invent encounters between its principal protagonists.
Although Guillén may not have known the *CC* directly, he most likely
knew one of its later manifestations, *Crónica particular del Cid* (1512),
Crónica popular del Cid (nineteen editions from 1494 to 1608), and Florián
de Ocampo's *Crónica de España* (1541) (Cazal 95; Arata xxxix–lx).[8] While
the ballads provided dialogue through lively, affective encounters for
Guillén's play, the narrative of either the *Crónica particular* or the *Crónica
ocampiana* is thought to have guided the playwright in the creation of
its narrative structure (Arata xlix). Additionally, minor details from two
episodes in the play reflect content found exclusively in the epic *MR*,
although it is likely that Guillén's knowledge of the narrative poem
arrived by an indirect route, such as an unidentified chronicle text or
ballads that are now lost to us (Arata xlix–l).

This preceding review is factual, but as with previous studies of the
play, it fails to note that these two medieval sources are in fact two
very different narratives.[9] In the chronicle version the hero is by nature
a loyal vassal of his king, portrayed as a mature, decisive, and distinguished monarch in harmony with the pre-existing, reverential narrative of the reign of Fernando I into which it has been integrated.[10] The
chronicle also incorporates elements from a monastic reworking of the
deeds of the mature Cid, perhaps best characterized as hagiographic
["de carácter hagiográfico"] (Viña Liste 2), generally identified as the
"Leyenda de Cardeña" ["Legend of Cardeña"], for its association with
the monastery of San Pedro de Cardeña. This pre-existing material,
along with the royal sponsorship of the chronicle and its composition
by one or more anonymous clerics combine to fashion a portrayal of
an obsequious Rodrigo that is decidedly unheroic and which contrasts
starkly with his assertive, independent-minded character in the
epic poem.

In the epic poem Rodrigo's loyalty lies first with his clan, essentially
his extended family and their allies, all of whom are disinclined to trust
or align themselves with the king. Ximena, who is as motivated as
Rodrigo by self-interest and at least acknowledges immediate family

ties as conditioners of her behaviour, ultimately seeks justice only for herself after Rodrigo kills her father in a pitched battle between the two families. Thus, even though the epic version is known to us through a manuscript that it shares with a late copy of the *CC*, its portrayal of Rodrigo and Ximena is reflective of a popular narrative of the deeds of a medieval warrior (non-monastic, anti-monarchical, independent of spirit and action) as opposed to a version of those same deeds elaborated under the watchful eyes of the monarchy (a hero who is obsequious, obedient, and reverential).

Therefore, and obviously, the assumption that the epic and chronicle versions are essentially the same leads to a misunderstanding of the reasons for the degree of variance in the character portrayals that are later reflected in three types of ballads: those based on the epic ("romances tradicionales"), the learned chronicles ("romances cronísticos"), and the "romances nuevos," a genre that has no direct link to either source and explored new scenarios related to the Cid narrative (Arata l–liii). By not acknowledging the medieval roots of these later versions of the Rodrigo narrative, audiences of the ballads and the play remain unaware of the rich resonances that can be derived from a familiarity with these earlier narrations. They also fail to appreciate the degree of adaptation evidenced in addressing the tastes and expectations of diverse audiences over time.

The dramatic tension of the play is based on the same motif that fueled the two medieval narratives, the killing of Count don Gómez de Gormaz by Rodrigo, the future husband of Ximena.[11] Yet, in the play the cause of the enmity between the two families is courtly, a slap from Ximena's father, el Conde, to the face of Diego Laínez, producing a stain of shame so profound that it can only be cleansed by the spilling of blood. Rodrigo is chosen for this task by his father and offers no resistance, even though he is already in love with Ximena. The encounter between Rodrigo and his father is based on a "romance nuevo," that is, a creative composition unencumbered by the legendary tradition, "Cvydando Diego Laynez" (Escobar 125–6; *Romancero general* 362). The second and only other ballad that Guillén incorporates into his portrayal of Rodrigo, "Pensatiuo estaua el Cid" (Escobar 126; *Romancero general* 69–70), is also a novel composition and it narrates Rodrigo's pre-duel thought process as he prepares himself to fight el Conde.[12] The first ballad describes a bizarre test of strength orchestrated by don Diego to ensure that Rodrigo is up to the task of defending the family honour. The second portrays Rodrigo as wary of his foe and vigilant in his preparations, although optimistic for his cause. Neither ballad has any precedent in the medieval legendary material, but both are concordant with Guillén's reformulation of Rodrigo as duty-bound and honour-driven and are fully incorporated into the play.

By way of contrast with his treatment of Rodrigo, among the four ballads that portray Ximena's plea for justice, Guillén chose not to deploy the one ballad that narrates the episode in accordance with the chronicle narrative, the only ballad of the four that presents her as composed and reasonable in her plea for justice, "De Rodrigo de Biuar" (Escobar 133-4). The ballad, like the chronicle episode it recreates, is exceptionally anodyne, lacking any kind of dramatic tension and unlikely to have ever been popular, that is, circulated orally. Also, this is the only ballad of the four in which Ximena proposes the idea of her marriage to Rodrigo as compensation for him killing her father, reasoning that Rodrigo's status will rise above that of other nobles in the kingdom, making a good and honourable marriage for herself, and asserting that the king should accede since it is God's will and because she would forgive Rodrigo for killing her father if he agreed to the marriage. All parties arrive to harmonious agreement and the ballad concludes as the marriage takes place. As in the chronicle text, the encounter depicted in this ballad is devoid of the dramatic tension conveyed in the epic narration and is no match for the other three ballads that Guillén does incorporate into his play. However, by excluding this ballad Guillén needed to devise another way to bring together Rodrigo and Ximena, which led to his decision to portray Rodrigo and Ximena as secretly in love from the start of the play.[13]

In both the epic poem and the chronicle text the marriage proposal represents the resolution of the conflict between the two warring families and offers the king a resolution to the dilemma he faces, his choice of either alienating the powerful Castilians over Ximena's demand for justice for the death of her father or denying Ximena her rightful justice. In the epic text it is also the episode's most affective moment, a powerful shock of surprise and release for the audience as well as for the king and his advisor. Stephano Arata assumes that the abandonment of the marriage proposal in the ballads takes place because the custom of allowing an orphaned girl to claim marriage to the killer of her father as compensation had fallen out of favour (lxii). This reasoning seems more than a little circular, and certainly not supported by any objective evidence. The episode as narrated in the *Crónica de Castilla* continues to be recreated in Spanish chronicles well into the sixteenth century, including Southey's English version of 1808 (5; book 1, para. 5), and so for some segment of the population at least, Ximena's marriage proposal continued to be relevant.

In the ballads that recreate Ximena's plea for justice and which Guillén does include in the play, Ximena's role has changed. She no longer tries to resolve the impasse for the king with a marriage proposal but is instead more insistent in her demand for justice, more critical of the king's tepid response, and more aggrieved in her victimhood. At some point in the evolution of the episode, the focus moved away from the marriage proposal as the principal affective moment, the surprise that captivated audiences and protagonists alike, and accentuated the plea for justice and the act of aggression that provoked it. Eventually, without Ximena's conciliatory gesture, the trajectory of the ballads led to the depiction of a wronged young woman whose increasingly strident demands for justice before an all-male court fell on deaf ears. The receptive king and his tutor, Ximena's complex and effective agency, and the process of the wheels of justice grinding out a satisfactory resolution have all been erased. By the time Guillén incorporated the ballads into his play, Ximena's demand for justice and her accumulated grievances are her sole focus.

These observations suggest that there is more to Guillén's artistry than simply deploying pre-existing ballads nearly verbatim, as Arata contends, "los romances quedan incrustados en la obra, con mínimas variants" ["the ballads are set into the work, with minimal variations"] (lxvii), or of complementing the dramatic structure of the play "insertados como tales en las diferentes situaciones dramáticas" ["inserted verbatim in different dramatic situations"] (xlv).[14] It is also more than a matter of the adaptation of ballad material in the way Françoise Cazal uses the term, to mean tweaking the expression of the ballads without changing their meaning (108), or to soften their impact (114), adding verses for a specific effect (116), or blending two sources (110), or in a general sense that might include all of the former (119). Sebold makes the better point when he observes that even when the expression of the ballad material is closest to its source, "el sentido de que [el autor] dota a la materia tradicional es muy distinto al que antes tenia" ["The meaning that the author gives to the traditional material is very different from that which it had previously"] (Sebold 218), which he attributes to the effects of the creation of a symbolic level of meaning, based on "las tradiciones ... del emblema y la literatura a lo divino" ["the traditions ... of emblems and of religious literature"] (242), namely the "galán divino" ["divine hero"] and "David español" ["Spanish David"] of his title. In other words, Guillén's creation of another level of meaning in the portrayal of Rodrigo reinforces the cultural and political tenets of the Counter-Reformation, reflecting these onto the traditional ballads incorporated into the play and infusing them with new meaning. These attributions to Guillén's artistry are correct in as much as they refer to the portrayal of Rodrigo, but in the case of Ximena, the role of the traditional ballads is more complex.

The fact that there are three separate and distinctive Cidian ballads depicting Ximena's pleas for the king to avenge the death of her father by punishing Rodrigo is a testament to the wide popularity of the episode. Including them in the play surely delighted the audience, especially in their representation of Ximena's enraged persona, projecting aggression, determination, even insult and deceit. Other ballads depict Ximena more in line with her characterization in the chronicles, as in "De Rodrigo de Biuar" (Escobar 133–4), or a "romance nuevo" such as "A Ximena y a Rodrigo" (Escobar 134–5), and with her otherwise conventional portrayal in the play, but Guillén chose not to deploy them.[15] In these three balladic eruptions, as it were, Guillén has positioned Ximena as a kind of female *parrhesiastes*, an admonisher of the king, speaking in truisms to the king and the audience about right governance, as in this sample from her first balladic sequence incorporated into the play late in the second act: "Si de Dios los reyes justos/la semejanza y el cargo/representan en la tierra/con los humildes humanos,/no debiera de ser Rey/bien temido y bien amado,/quien desmaya la justicia/y esfuerza los desacatos" ["If just kings represent on this Earth to humble humans the likeness and the rule of God, he should not be king, either feared or loved, who neglects justice and empowers offence"] (*MC*, vv. 1741–8).

Ximena is speaking truth to power and in the process is risking her reputation, exposing herself to ridicule and mockery and so in danger of diminishing her own social status, as we will examine in brief. As Foucault points out in his analysis of the *parrhesiastic* role of Ion, the title character in the play by Euripides, *parrhesia* is not a right given equally to all Athenian citizens, but only to those who are especially prestigious due to their family and their birth. In this sense Ximena is the kind of individual who is valuable to a monarchy, just as with Ion in Euripides's play and Rodrigo in the medieval *Mocedades*, since her social status and courage empower her to explain to the king his shortcomings as a ruler (following Foucault 51). In Ximena's case, the daughter of the king's champion and a count, her social status grants her access to the royal audience she seeks on three separate occasions, but it is also the source of her anxiety as she seeks to uphold her family's honour. We might also take a moment to consider the possibility that Guillén portrayed Ximena in this way, that is lodging a legitimate criticism against the king for not dispensing justice against a subject he holds most dear, in this case his prize vassal and defender of the realm, a banner-carrying member of the highest nobility, yet doing so in her conflicted state of having to demand retribution against Rodrigo, the man she loves, as a way to voice criticism of the king, in this case Felipe III, or of the monarchy in a more general way, but to also give the audience a mechanism for discounting it.[16]

The dismissal of Ximena's charged speech is not something we need imagine for the audience; it takes place on the stage. The most studied of these ballads, "En Burgos está el buen Rey" (Escobar 131), is the last of the three ballads deployed and represents the culmination of the process of discrediting Ximena in her quest for justice. The ballad itself bears the traces of an oral evolution that includes the mingling of at least one additional narrative tradition with Ximena's plea (Carberry 45–53, Montaner, "Las quejas" 483). The version in Escobar's collection is most likely the one deployed by Guillén, although it includes variants that can be ascribed to its oral trajectory (Cazal 115–17). The accusation wielded by Ximena mentions only in passing the killing of el Conde, her father. Her main charge is Rodrigo's subsequent aggressive stalking of her, clearly an extremely egregious act and accusation.[17] The ballad is magnificently coherent in its ferocity:

> Cada día que amanece/veo quien mató a mi padre,
> caballero en un caballo,/y en su mano un gavilán,
> A mi casa de placer,/donde alivio mi pesar,
> curioso, libre y ligero,/mira, escucha, viene y va,
> y por hacerme despecho/dispara a mi palomar
> flechas que a los vientos tira,/y en el corazón me dan.
> Mátame mis palomicas/criadas y por criar,
> la sangre que sale dellas/me ha salpicado el brial.
> Enbiéselo a decir,/envióme amenazar
> con que ha de dejar sin vida/cuerpo que sin alma está.
> Rey que no hace justicia/no debría de reinar,
> ni pasear en caballo,/ni con la reina folgar.
> ¡Justicia, buen Rey, justicia!   (vv. 1973–97)

Every new day that rises, I see the one who killed my father,/a knight on a horse, and a sparrow hawk in his hand,/to my country cottage,/where I go to forget my troubles,/curious, free and guiltless,/he looks, listens, comes and goes,/and to spite me,/he shoots at my dovecote,/arrows that he shoots into the air,/and they strike me in the heart./He kills my lovely doves, adults and chicks,/the blood that flows from them has stained my apron./I sent word for him to stop, he sent me threats/that he will take the life/from a body that has no soul./The king who does not do justice/ should not reign,/nor parade on horseback,/nor lie with the queen./Justice, good king, justice!

As in the case of the play's previous two ballads dedicated to Ximena's plea, here she demands that the king act, asserting that any king who does not dispense justice does not deserve royal prerogatives. The king ponders his situation, here again concerned about provoking a revolt if he punishes the Cid, not from the Castilians, as in the epic text, but from his "Cortes" ["courtiers"]. And yet, if he does not dispense justice, God will hold him to account. The king unilaterally decides to send a letter to the Cid summoning him to court. The response to the letter provides a brief glimpse of Rodrigo's overbearing personality as he chides his father for not voluntarily revealing to him the contents of the king's letter. When his father tells him to stay home, the Cid defies him.

It is not an entirely coherent composition. Several of the narrative elements are not as fully developed as in the other versions of Ximena's plea, such as her status as an orphan, the killing of her father, the additional privileges that a derelict king should no longer enjoy, but this brevity seems to create a space for the novel accusation against Rodrigo of stalking and violent aggression. The presence of this accusation has no precedent in the epic narratives dedicated to the Cid, and traditionally it has been attributed to a mingling of narrative motifs from unrelated stories, a process that scholars have insisted on calling "contamination," in this case the mingling of the story of the legendary doña Lambra with that of Ximena.

Lambra is a nefarious female figure associated in epic narrative with the deaths of the flower of Castilian nobility, the "siete infantes de Lara" ["seven princes of Lara"], in an act of revenge for her humiliation after an act of sexual provocation ended in violence (Carberry 34–45, for a review). Lambra's response was to claim that the infantes had threatened her with sexual aggression and that she was a widow with no one to protect her (her husband was away at the time). The ballad tradition articulates the specific threats that Lambra attributes to the infantes, and it is this version that scholars assume found its way into Ximena's accusations against Rodrigo: "y cebarían sus halcones/dentro de mi palomar,/y me forzarían mis damas/casadas y por casar" ["and they would bait their hawks/inside my dovecote/and they would rape my ladies/married and maiden"] (Carberry 47).

For these accusations of sexual aggression to have been transferred from the infantes to the iconic Cid makes sense in a context in which the legendary infantes and doña Lambra had ceased to reside in the collective imaginations of the purveyors of ballads and their audiences, and in which the Cid's legendary life, his deeds, and the personal traits traditionally associated with him were no longer prominent. It also seems pertinent to recall that Lambra's accusations are false, the infantes never made the threats that she attributes to them. They represent the workings of her fetid imagination, which she unleashes in an effort to emasculate her husband and incite him to avenge her shame. Surely these falsehoods, in their migration from Lambra's lament to Ximena's, were understood by Guillén as false accusations against Rodrigo, made in a desperate attempt by Ximena to incite the king to action, much as Lambra used them to shame her husband into taking revenge against the infantes.

In incorporating this ballad into the play, Guillén includes most of it (Cazal 114–17) but makes immediately clear that Ximena's claims about Rodrigo's violent behaviour are outrageous and not attached to reality. As with Ximena's previous two pleas, the context in which the ballad appears is very much the matter. The scene begins with the depiction of the king negotiating his response to a challenge delivered by an ambassador sent by the king of Aragón, to decide the fate of the disputed city of Calahorra by single combat. For this contest, he has chosen Rodrigo as his champion. While in these discussions, the king is informed that Ximena has requested an audience with him, to which he responds irascibly: "Tiene del Conde Lozano/la arrogancia y la impaciencia" ["She has from el Conde Lozano (like him)/his arrogance and his impatience"] (vv. 1935–6), followed by irritation at her ongoing demands: "Siempre la tengo a mis pies,/descompuesta y querellosa" ["She is always at my feet/disheveled and whining" (vv. 1937–8). As in "Grande rumor se leuanta" (Escobar 130), Ximena is described by the king as a kind of female grotesque, the unruly woman who disrupts the affairs of state and the king's desire for order.[18] When Diego Laínez responds with a stirring banality, "Es honrada y es hermosa" ["She is honourable and she is beautiful"], the king continues serving up slights "Importuna también es" ["she is also irksome"] (vv. 1939–40).

This dialogue serves a dual purpose. In it we see that Diego Laínez wants to soften the impact of Ximena's insistent pleas to the king, since he is aware that she and Rodrigo have managed to preserve their love in spite of the challenging circumstances. It also underlines the risk that Ximena is taking in leveraging her status to continue to admonish the king and present increasingly alarming accusations. Even though the accusations against Rodrigo become certifiably untrue, the admonishments to the king are verifiably accurate. The king has shown himself to be reluctant to punish Rodrigo because of his dependence on him as a valuable warrior and as his champion. Ximena's tirade is an act of *parrhesia* in the sense that the person accused is more powerful than the accuser and that the accused, the king, may retaliate against Ximena (following Foucault 53). The king does seem to be at his wits' end, fed up with the constant criticism and demands for justice from Ximena, which he sees as extreme irritants to his addressing matters of state. We never do see the consequences to which the king's emotions are building, since the situation is assuaged when Arias Gonzalo informs the king that Ximena and Rodrigo are in love and that, although she may well continue to insist on demanding that the king punish Rodrigo, her interests would be best served by promoting their marriage (vv. 1947–55). The two components of Ximena's plea, the personal and the political, are not equal. One is true, the king has been delinquent in administering justice; the other is untrue, Rodrigo is not a sexual predator. The conflating of the two in one balladic sequence may have allowed Guillén to level a legitimate criticism of the monarchy, while masking his intention by associating it with an easily dismissed fantasy.[19]

Ximena then enters the scene at court and begins her lament, following closely the ballad on which it is based. In this context – their enduring love, their desire for society's approval, the feigned insistence on justice – the charges she levels against Rodrigo of stalking and violent aggression against her ring hollow. Diego Laínez tries to make sense of what he has just heard, suggesting that Ximena might have dreamed these things ("sospecho que lo soñáis" ["I believe you dreamed it"], v. 2002), her crying has blurred her memory ("si os desvanece el llorar/ lo habréis soñado esta noche" ["if crying has weakened you/you must have dreamed it last night"], vv. 2004–5). Ximena's accusations suggest a faltering moral compass, an ever-more desperate attempt to force the king's hand and so recover her honour in the public eye, while in her heart she continues to love Rodrigo. Her response to don Diego's assertion that Rodrigo is on pilgrimage to Santiago and could not have done the things she claims, is to say that it happened before he left (v. 2013), and then in a telling rebuttal: "Ya en mi ofensa, que estoy loca/solo falta que digáis" ["so to insult me, that I am crazy/is all that's left for you to say"] (vv. 2015–16). She seems to sense that her claims are beyond the pale, and that her desperate act reflects poorly on herself. Just as Ximena speaks these words, a page arrives to report that Rodrigo has been killed in battle. Ximena reacts as expected, with a knot in her throat and anguish in her heart, but once she learns that it was a ruse meant to trick her into revealing her true feelings, she revives her demand for justice by offering a reward for Rodrigo's head. Another ruse will follow, and through it Ximena again reveals her true feelings, leading her to accept Rodrigo's profession of love and marriage.

Apart from her three pleas for justice, which come late in the play, Ximena's character is similar to Rodrigo. She is by nature circumspect and self-sacrificing, very much in accord with the cultural current of the time, a "paragon of acceptable social conduct" (Agheana 35). Her motivation to seek justice for the killing of her father is not based on her personal desires, but on the expectations of society that she alone carries. Her true desire is to marry Rodrigo, even though circumstances have conspired to lead her to question herself and her motives. She is heroic in her resolve to sublimate her personal desires to the social expectations of her time, much more so than Rodrigo, who is able to avenge his father's shame and to pursue his love interest, to have his cake and eat it too, so to speak. In the medieval legend and the ballad tradition a case has been made for Ximena as a heroic "femme impudique," as someone who is sexually forward and, in this way, conspires to control the hero (Montgomery, "Horatius" 547). This is not the case in the play since none of her pleas for justice are meant to compel Rodrigo to marry her. This disjuncture between Ximena in the ballads, her ferocity of spirit, her sense of righteousness and implacable demand for justice, and her character as it is revealed in the course of the play, has led to the suggestion that the medieval Ximena has been erased: "the original, independent and valiant Jimena is sadly missing" from the play (Ratcliffe 263). The earlier Ximena is very much present in the play, yet the play itself makes it apparent that her balladic discourse does not represent her true feelings, nullifying her fervor and aggression. The accusations of stalking and sexual aggression against the Cid are not suppressed, but they are spoken in a context in which they make no sense. The legendary Cid of epic and ballad is the one who is absent from the play, as Guillén opted to incorporate only new ballads in his portrayal ("Cuydando Diego Laynez," "Pensativo estaba el Cid," Escobar 125–6), ballads that portray a cautious and introspective obedient son, not the aggressive, self-confident, independent-minded warrior of the medieval *Mocedades de Rodrigo*.

The figurative emasculation of the young Cid and the exposure and subsequent ridicule of Ximena's assertive self are two sides of the same coin. The Counter-Reformation ethos of the play would not countenance a young noble challenging the authority of the king, as the Rodrigo of the medieval epic does as a matter of course. Nor would it tolerate the portrayal of a young woman, even one of exalted nobility, successfully taking charge of the disastrous situation in which her family finds itself after her father's death and providing a clueless king with the solution to a matter of state that he was unable to resolve for himself. In both cases, the displacement of the epic hero and the mockery made of Ximena's balladic protestations, their revival is in part an exercise in demonstrating that they have no place in the early modern state. Rodrigo's masculine virility is very much on display in the medieval epic and even more explicitly in the balladic references to his sexual aggression, introduced in the play in a way that extinguishes their power. Ximena's protestations, her wagging tongue, is the female counterpoint, and it too is silenced, much like the scolds or shrews of late sixteenth-century England that provide the real-life context for the taming of a more familiar shrew, Shakespeare's Kate (Boose 184–5).[20] Ximena's appropriation of the role of *parrhesiastes* in the *Mocedades del Cid*, her usurpation of Rodrigo's phallic authority by way of her unruly member, also ends in a form of castration, her silencing through marriage (following Boose 204).

In the way of confirmation of these findings, we find additional evidence of the unique treatment of Ximena in the *Mocedades del Cid-Segunda comedia*, the second part of Guillén's two-play sequence on the young Cid. Like Ximena, Urraca Fernando is a historical female figure whose legendary reputation suffered as the ballad tradition evolved. She was the daughter of King Fernando I, and the sister of his sons, future kings all, Sancho, García, and Alfonso. Medieval chronicles portray her as an outspoken victim, first of her father's neglect when he partitioned his kingdom among his three sons and left her with nothing, and secondly when her brothers, first García and then Sancho, attempt to take by force of arms the city of Zamora that was left to her by a repentant Fernando on his deathbed. Her troubles seem to resolve when her brother, King Sancho II of Castile, is stabbed in the back by Vellido Dolfos during Sancho's siege of Zamora, but legend subsequently links her to the regicide through the suggestion of a secret promise of sexual favour to the assassin. In the ballad tradition Urraca is also portrayed as Ximena's rival for Rodrigo's affection and, as the loser in that rivalry, as an embittered and forlorn *infanta*.

Two ballads attributed to Urraca, best known as "Morir vos queredes, padre" and "Afuera, afuera, Rodrigo," are prominent in the play. In the first ballad, as her father lay dying, Urraca describes her future as a landless woman: "Irm' he yo por esas tierras como una mujer errada,/y este mi cuerpo daría a quien bien se me antojara:/a los moros por dineros y a los cristianos de gracia;/de lo que ganar pudiere haré bien por vuestra alma" ["I will go through these lands like a wanton woman,/and this my body I would give to whomever I well please:/to Moors for money and to Christians for free;/anything I might earn I will use for the good of your soul"] (Díaz-Mas 76). Yet, in the play, it is not Urraca who voices the ballad, but Rodrigo, who does so as he reminds Sancho that he swore an oath to honour the partitioning of his father's kingdom, including the designation of Zamora for Urraca, thus normalizing Urraca's rebuke as part of a dialogue about honour and the sacredness of oaths. Additionally, Urraca's more extreme protestations of her putative landless depravity are excluded from the play, and the single consequence of her being left without a landed inheritance is not posed as a threat but as a question: "¿Havré de ir de tierra en tierra/como una mugger errada?" ["Must I go from place to place/like a wanton woman?"] (88).

The second ballad, "Afuera, afuera, Rodrigo," is traditionally seen as Urraca's rejection of the Cid after he chose Ximena's love over hers. There is nothing patently immoral or scandalous in the ballad itself, and it is part of a larger discussion in the play between Urraca and Rodrigo in which she accuses him of abandoning her in the defence of Zamora. Rodrigo does his best to answer her charges of his rejection of her love and of breaking his vow to King Fernando to honour the king's decision to grant Zamora to Urraca. In this way, the ballad material, originally concerned only with love lost, is diffused into the wider context of the defence of Zamora and Rodrigo's sense of duty.

A ballad that is incorporated nearly verbatim into the play and is scandalous in its treasonous implications is one is which Rodrigo compels King Alfonso VI to swear under oath and upon pain of death, that he had no role in the regicide of his brother, King Sancho II ("La jura de Santa Gadea," Díaz-Mas 89-93). In the ballad, the Cid's temerity in demanding that Alfonso swear such an oath before him and the assembled courtiers leads to the king's angry denunciation of the Cid and banishment. In the play, Rodrigo and Alfonso scheme to perform the oath ceremony as a public exoneration of Alfonso, in order to pre-emptively squelch any rumors that might arise concerning possible suspicions about Alfonso's role in his brother's death. The oath that Alfonso is compelled to speak is essentially the same as in the ballad tradition, but the play has already made clear that Alfonso had no role in his brother's assassination, and so the oath, performed as political theatre, loses its gravity before it is spoken (157–8).

The singularity of Guillén's portrayal of Ximena becomes even clearer through a reading of Corneille's *Le Cid*. While Guillén incorporates three balladic pleas for justice by Ximena, Corneille recreates just one, a combination of the first and second pleas in Guillén's play. Ximena's more scandalous accusations of sexual aggression against Rodrigo are not part of the play. The French audiences were most likely not aware of the wider Spanish balladic tradition that Guillén felt compelled to incorporate into his play, giving Corneille license to exclude the more extreme of the balladic accusations against Rodrigo and so avoid even more scandal, especially in the mocking and shaming of Ximena.

Guillén de Castro's *Mocedades del Cid* has been understood as a play that relies on legendary ballads for the characterization of its main protagonist, the young Rodrigo. While there may be echoes of these legendary ballads in the play, the two ballads that are more fully incorporated are not based on legend, they are "romances nuevos." These compositions help fashion the Counter-Reformation portrayal of Rodrigo that Guillén crafted for his play, a Rodrigo who is thoughtful, self-abnegating, and obedient. It is only in the portrayal of Ximena that Guillén deploys legendary ballads. In their performance, Ximena is depicted in a kind of post-medieval fury that evolved from her traditional plea for justice, but that over time had become more desperate and aggrieved. Ximena makes her case that if the king will not dispense justice for the killing of her father, then he is no king, he does not deserve the privileges of his station, and God will judge him harshly. She also accuses Rodrigo of stalking her and recounts acts of bloody aggression against her that resonate with sexuality. These accusations are incompatible with the heroic standards of Counter-Reformation Spain, and to mitigate their effect Guillén contextualizes Ximena's pleas in a way that ensures their dismissal, by the other characters, the audience, and even by Ximena herself. This technique allowed Guillén to incorporate into his play widely popular ballads, surely to the satisfaction of his audience, and yet also normalize the Counter-Reformation representation of Rodrigo and, ultimately, Ximena. These co-protagonists emerge from the play as paragons of virtue, but Ximena's unruly pleas also allow the audience an opportunity to delight in the evocation of an earlier time, when a king would be called to task by a powerful woman demanding justice and the most rapacious behaviour was attributed to heroic figures.

Conclusion

In concluding this work, we might start with the insight that a narrative like Rodrigo's *mocedades* is not generated by a lone author with an idea for a story. It draws its content from previous narratives that were successful, with multiple versions that evolved over time, and as social and political conditions change, as one nation rises above others, the nationality, the language, the allegiance, and even the name of the protagonist can migrate or change. An example examined in these pages is the Roland-Bernardo-Fernán González-Fierabras-Rodrigo continuum (or in another order, we can't really know for certain), which spans cultures and languages, is capable of idealizing former enemies, and privileges heroic acts over actors. Equally compelling is the right of passage of Rodrigo, with echoes of the youthful deeds of the Irish epic hero Cú Chulainn. The two protagonists are culturally and geographically distant, yet the parallels between their initiations into the warrior world encouraged poets and audiences and, in turn, us to think of them in tandem. Tales such as these must have been so engrossing that their audiences assimilated them, carrying them along as they mutated and evolved over centuries and across cultures. In the face of this evidence, it is hard to make a case for the prominence of one version of a story over another, or to even pose the question of the originality or the authenticity of any particular manifestation of a narrative. Manuscripts are concrete, and oral narrative is fluid, by its very nature in continual evolution, but there is a dependency of one on the other, and the vibrancy of these tales and the mutations they engender suggest audiences that are diverse and mobile. The author or compiler of a manuscript is not responsible for the tale being recorded, only for its latest, and likely not last, recreation.

Another indication of the fluidity of this process of renewal, of the ability of a narrative like that of Rodrigo's youth, to adapt to specific social and political situations, and to rapidly incorporate and assimilate new material, is the appearance of Saint Lazarus on the pilgrim road to Santiago. This leper-saint and the knights who lived through his suffering and the teaching of Christ that it elicited were in all likelihood not associated with the pilgrim road to Santiago until after 1291, subsequent to the fall of Acre and the Islamic recovery of the Holy Land, when the Lazarite knights retreated to France. If so, then in a period of some nine or ten years until the composition of the chronicle version of the Rodrigo narrative, the figure of Saint Lazarus had replaced Saint James, the more traditional patron of pilgrims to Santiago, who had earlier rendered his assistance to King Fernando in the historical siege of Coimbra. In this short span of time, Rodrigo is newly imagined as an exemplar of Christian charity and the beneficiary of the leper-saint's gratitude, earning himself divine recognition and a guarantee of future invincibility. The episode is narrated in both chronicle and poem with minor differences, and later again in early modern drama where its implications are even more consequential. By identifying a specific time frame for the reformulation of this episode, a stunningly clear picture emerges of the torrid pace of adaptation of the narrative and a similarly fluid notion of composition.

The critical reception of the poem has suffered to some extent because scholars have been frustrated in their attempts to identify a narrative arc in the poem, or any sense of narrative cohesion. The manuscript copy of the poem is imperfect, and as such transitions are sometimes brusque and context is lacking for a few of the episodes. But the poem exhibits coherence in other ways. The many affective encounters in the poem are a case in point. These begin well before the emergence of Rodrigo, and a few of the early examples are protagonized by Ximena. Most prominent however, are the affective encounters that involve Rodrigo speaking truth to power. Although his behaviour has been characterized as rebellious, and it does in some instances suggest an unwillingness to bend to authority, more to the point is the right behaviour that gives power to his truth-telling.

At twelve years of age, Rodrigo is bursting with excitement at the prospect of his first battle and refuses to be excluded from combat against the forces of Count don Gómez de Gormaz, Ximena's father and the enemy of his clan and loyal vassals. Later, Rodrigo refuses to go along with his father's evasion of responsibility for the capture of Ximena's brothers. He instead acknowledges that Ximena and her sisters have no fault in their father's aggression and that as newly orphaned young women they are in desperate need of their captive brothers. Rodrigo also refuses to consummate the marriage to Ximena imposed on him, or to serve King Fernando until he has proven his manhood by winning five battles in the field of combat. He refuses to pay tribute to a king to whom he has not sworn fealty and who did not participate in the battlefield victory over five Muslim lords. He justifies this refusal by giving respective portions to the poor, to the Church, and to the men who fought with him. Nor will he hand over his captive Muslim king, reminding the querulous king who is soliciting him that the warrior code of conduct does not allow him to dishonour a noble captive in this way. Other examples of Rodrigo's right behaviour follow along these same lines, they play out in arresting fashion, as words and deeds combine to create truly memorable moments of narrative impact. These moments, the right behaviour they portray, and the matter-of-fact way in which Rodrigo continually speaks truth to power bind the narrative together and constitute its coherence.

We know these examples of Rodrigo's conduct are exemplary because the narrative finds ways to reward them. When Rodrigo demands to fight alongside his father and uncles against Count don Gómez, he strikes the fatal blow that kills the count and captures his sons. When Ximena's brothers are handed over to her after Rodrigo's intervention, she convinces them not to take revenge on Rodrigo's family and instead takes her plea directly to the king, which leads to her marriage to Rodrigo and the resolution of the dispute between their families. In response to Rodrigo's refusal to share his hard-won battlefield booty with King Fernando and instead reward the men who fought with him, three hundred of Fernando's vassals annul their fealty to him and swear allegiance to Rodrigo. Rodrigo's charitable treatment of a desperate leper on the pilgrim road to Santiago leads to a promise of Christ's support and invincibility in his single combat for Calahorra. The tough love that Rodrigo shows his nephew Pero Mudo, a form of truth-telling, brings his nephew to his senses and sets him on the path to success as he promises his allegiance to Rodrigo and is rewarded by a return to his good graces.

Another way to appreciate the affective response to Rodrigo's truth-telling and the right behaviour that supports it, is to acknowledge the efforts that were made to diminish it. In its earliest manifestation, in the fight against the Frankish invasion, long before it was associated with Rodrigo, Lucas de Tuy's Bernardo del Carpio was compelled to join forces with the Muslim king Marsil in defence of the kingdom of Asturias because their king was unwilling to do battle against the army of Charlemagne. The succinct nature of the Latin prose chronicle does not allow for an analysis of how Bernardo responded in speech to his king, but he did respond with rage to Charlemagne's demand that Alfonso pay him homage and rushed to join forces with Marsil against the invading Franks, winning him the praise of Lucas and his audience. This narrative of Bernardo's right action and most likely defiant response to his king's acquiescence, was transformed by Rodrigo Jiménez de Rada, who for reasons of his proximity to the monarchy credited King Alfonso with the defence of his kingdom, explicitly denying a prominent role for Bernardo. Likewise, the prose *Crónica de Castilla* narrates essentially the same episodes and events as the verse *Mocedades*, but that royal effort portrays the needy and unmoored King Fernando of the poem as a paragon of royal privilege and authority, and Rodrigo as his valuable, but ultimately subservient, vassal. Guillén's portrayal of Rodrigo and Ximena takes even more license in not only ennobling the king and his high-status courtiers by emasculating Rodrigo, but also in mocking and humiliating Ximena, whose demands for justice and critique of a monarch unwilling to dispense it resonate with the same truths that characterized Rodrigo in the medieval epic.

In the medieval *mocedades*, Rodrigo's most salient characteristic is his willingness to speak truth to power. While the mature Cid, in spite of his heroic attributes and success, is pliant and ultimately acquiesces to his king's demands, the young Rodrigo emerges from a distinct tradition of defiant protagonists to take on the mantel of the true *parrhesiastes*. This portrayal is contrary to the representations of legendary warriors we find in the texts of Spanish historiography and the concepts of power that they articulate. Despite the messaging of royal chronicles and the dominant discourse of Counter-Reformation Spain, the legend of the young Rodrigo survived as a counternarrative, one in which the hero is a kind of recurring image, the legendary warrior whose courage, singular merits, and right-thinking empower him to speak truth to power and to model for others how they might do the same.

Rodrigo's legendary life in medieval chronicle, poem, and in Renaissance ballad and drama, also confirms its vitality, its adaptability, its appeal, and perhaps most importantly, the lasting impact of its two powerful protagonists, Rodrigo and Ximena. Their relationship, born in turmoil and anointed in self-preservation, echoes through time in a way that other Spanish medieval epic narratives never would. The mature Cid, Fernán González, Bernardo del Carpio, Siete infantes, were all cast aside as they emerged into the modern age. It may well have been their pairing that ultimately carried them forward, but the other aspects of the narrative of Rodrigo's youth explored in the preceding pages make a case for the power of an aesthetic principle based on the depiction of affective encounters engendered by a willingness to challenge inept authority and exemplify right behaviour, and through their portrayal, the exploration of a deep and abiding humanity.

Notes

1 The Legendary Response to Charlemagne in Spain

1 This chapter has been substantially revised from an earlier publication written for another context ("Charlemagne as a Creative Force").
2 Throughout his career, Ramón Menéndez Pidal sought to link historical events and the *Cantar de Mio Cid*, perhaps most forcefully in *La España del Cid*. Subsequent scholarship recognizes the literary aspects of the Spanish epic, yet in general continues to assume an intrinsic link to the historical events of the time. Examples are innumerable.
3 In the entry for the year 778, Bernhard Scholz with Barbara Rogers offer additional contextual details that contradict some of Lewis's assertions. They explain that the conspiracy against Umayyad rule failed

> because of distrust among the partners in the revolt. Sulaiman in the end faced the whole Umayyad army alone. He therefore sought help from Charles, but this proved to be more of a handicap. Sulaiman took Saragossa and tried to hand the city over to Charles. This outraged Muslim public opinion and Charles decided to return (not because of the Saxon revolt, news of which reached him only at Autun). Abd ar-Rahman recaptured Saragossa, and Sulaiman was murdered as a traitor to the Muslim cause. (*Royal Frankish Annals* 185n1)

Scholz, with Rogers, and Lewis, all agree on the significance of the role of Sulaiman ibn al-Arabi in inducing Charlemagne to venture into Spain.
4 Molly Robinson Kelly takes this observation one step further, noting that the attribution of the defeat of Charlemagne to the terrain (and to the light armament of the enemy) is echoed in the *Song of Roland*, and asserts that both authors believe that it constitutes "an unjust and discourteous use of space – a failure to play by the rules of the game – and that consequently Roncevaux should not be seen as a defeat for Charlemagne" (141).
5 Dámaso Alonso discovered the text and presented it in a substantial study that includes a transcription and six distinct photographic plate

reproductions, still widely available. For a review of the text of the *Nota* and its interpretation by Alonso and Menéndez Pidal, see Barton Sholod 157–62. Citations of the text are from the transcription by Alonso (9).

6 The editor of the most recent edition of the *Historia Silensis*, Juan A. Estévez Sola, suggests that a specific date of composition is elusive, "antes de 1118," or "antes de 1124," "o incluso … antes de 1135," are the best estimates, "poco más puede saberse" (76). Simon Barton and Richard Fletcher propose a date of composition for the *Silensis*, "certainly after 1109 and probably before 1118" (9) and a possible audience for the work (23), as well as a synopsis on the passage related to Charlemagne that highlights the author's dismissive attitude towards the French (20–1). They do not include in their English translation the passages examined here.

7 The author's indirect reference to assertions by the Franks may well be in response to Einhard's *Vita*, in which he states that Charlemagne crossed the Pyrennes and accepted the surrender of all the towns and castles that he passed "saltuque Pyrinei superato, omnibus, quae adierat, oppidis atque castellis in deditionem acceptis" (Einhard 54). In a subsequent reference, Einhard states that Charlemagne conquered Aquitaine, Gascony, and the entire Pyrenees region as far south as the river Ebro (66). Barton and Fletcher make reference to the author's inspiration in specific phrases of Einhard, as well as in the overall design of the *Vita* (17).

8 The reference to the offer by ibn al-Arabi suggests that the author was also familiar with the *Royal Frankish Annals*.

9 The reference to Charlemagne's palace at Aachen and the thermal baths may be slightly anachronistic, as the palace complex was a ten-year work in progress, becoming the king's permanent residence in the mid-790s. "Aachen's thermal springs had been channeled by the Romans to make a large, colonnaded bath whose waters stayed at a comfortable sixty-five degrees" (Lewis 296). Einhard tells us that the king enjoyed the steam of natural hot springs, which is why he built his palace at Aachen and spent the last years of his life there without interruption (86).

10 Francisco Bautista makes a similar point by highlighting elements of the invasion episode in the *Silensis* reflected in other sources, such as the Franks' corruption by gold and Charlemagne's fervent desire to return to his baths in Aachem (71–2). See also Justo Pérez de Urbel and Atilano González de Zorrilla 49-52.

11 The reign of Alfonso II of Asturias (791–842) does not coincide with Charlemagne's invasion of Spain in 778, as noted by Louis Chalon (64).

12 This and all other translations into English are mine, unless noted otherwise.

13 Bernardo's alliance with Charlemagne after leading the slaughter of his rearguard is confounding. It may represent the conflation of several

narrative traditions, including one involving Bernardo in the Ribagorza region of Spain (Bautista 60–5).

14 The *Pseudo-Turpin* is the more exacting modern name for the Latin chronicle known as *Historia Karoli Magni et Rholandi*, a feigned eyewitness account of the military campaigns in which Charlemagne conquered all of Spain and Galicia, by an anonymous author posing as Bishop Turpin of Rheims, a contemporary of Charlemagne. The original version of the *Turpin* was most likely composed in the decade of 1140–50, although subsequent redactions continued for centuries. The *Pseudo-Turpin* constitutes Book 4 of a five-part composition known as the *Book of Saint James*, written by another anonymous author, this time a pseudo Pope Calixtus II. This false attribution accounts for the identification of its oldest manuscript as the *Codex Calixtinus*, in the cathedral archive of Santiago de Compostela. The *Book* is an instrument for glorifying the apostle and his shrine at Compostela, and more specifically for inciting the faithful of France to make the pilgrimage to that shrine. The actual authors are thought to be French Cluniacs (Smyser 1–3), or a resident of Poitiers (Bautista 82).

15 Juan Fernández Valverde notes that Jiménez de Rada "es un magnífico compendiador que resume con mano maestra otros textos" ["is a wonderful abridger (editor), who summarizes with great skill other texts"] (xl).

16 This secret embassy sent by Alfonso to Charlemagne is apocryphal, although an alliance did occur at a later date, as indicated by Chalon (64). In another context, Einhard in his *Vita* asserts that King Alfonso referred to himself as Charles's vassal in their communications: "Adeo namque Hadefonsum Galleciae atque Asturicae regem sibi societate devinxit, ut is, cum ad eum vel litteras vel legatos mitteret, non aliter se apud illum quam proprium suum appellari iuberet" (68; chap. 16). As part of a much broader thesis, Anne Latowsky references the passage from Einhard and suggests that we should consider this unsubstantiated claim of submission by Alfonso "metonymically," as a kind of shorthand used by Einhard to establish the western extreme of Charlemagne's geography (26).

17 It is interesting to see the archbishop distinguishing between fact and fiction from among legendary accounts of Charlemagne's invasion of Spain. The narrative contained in the *Pseudo-Turpin* is truly outlandish and would be an easy target for anyone questioning the exploits of Charlemagne described therein – whether he heard it from jongleurs directly, or attributed it to them from a written source like the *Turpin*.

18 More detail and analysis on this topic are provided in chap. 3.

19 For this work I use the more familiar, conventional title of *Poema*, while textual references in this chapter will be taken from the *Libro de Fernán*

González, with corresponding verse numbers from the "Transcripción paleográfica" (135–225), with minor changes to the transcription to facilitate word recognition.

20 Alonso Zamora Vicente, in a note to v. 134 (41), links the mention of a written source for the reference to seven dead kings and potentates to the *Pseudo-Turpin*, but I have not been able to confirm a direct correlation, as in, for example 90; chap. 31. Pelayo de Oviedo's copy of the *Liber historiae Francorum* does contain an interpolation identifying seven warrior potentates "patricios potentissimos" who accompanied Charlemagne in his fabled conquest of Spain (Bautista 77).

21 Zamora Vicente identifies the first battle as the Battle of Roncesvalles of "poemas franceses" ["French poems"] (41, note to v. 134), although only the second battle takes place in the Pyrenees: "al puerto de Gitarea fizieron luego tornada,/ … por los de Aspa fueron luego torcidos" (vv. 138b–39b), places identified by López Guil as "los desfiladeros de Roncesvalles" ["the defiles of Roncesvalles"] and "El paso de Aspa está en la actual provincial de Huesca, cercano por el oeste a Somport y al sur de Alcren" ["The pass of Aspe is in the province of Huesca, near Somport to the west and to the south of Alcren,"] in her notes to vv. 138b and 139b (*Libro de Fernán González* 393).

22 Zamora Vicente links the identification of these warriors to their role in the *Pseudo-Turpin* (107; note to v. 352). In fact, the Latin identifiers added above were taken from the *Pseudo-Turpin*: Engelenus (dux Aquitanie) (67; chap. 13), Gandelbodus (rex Frisie) and Salomon socius Estulti (68; chap. 13). However, in the same way that the *Pseudo-Turpin* incorporates protagonists from a variety of French *Chansons de geste* into a single narrative, it is possible that the author of the *Fernán González* is recollecting them in a similar fashion, from his familiarity with more than one epic narrative and not directly from the *Pseudo-Turpin*.

23 Arguments regarding the date and provenance of the extant manuscript text of the narrative of the young Cid's deeds are reviewed in the bilingual edition of the poem (Bailey, Introduction 5–8).

24 In the *Crónica de Castilla*, the invasion of France is narrated in twelve paragraphs ("Fernando I el Magno" paras. 99–110; chaps. 21–2). In the *Mocedades de Rodrigo* the invasion episode is found in verses 804–1225.

25 One hundred thousand Moorish mounted warriors are called up by Moorish kings, vassals of King Fernando, for the invasion of France in the *Crónica de Castilla* ("Fernando I el Magno" para. 101; chap. 21), but not in the *MR*.

26 The pope does threaten a crusade against Spain for refusing his demands in the chronicle versions (*CC*, "Fernando I el Magno" para. 99; chap. 21), but the Spaniards take the initiative and invade France.

27 The degree of influence exerted by the Bernardo narratives on the *Mocedades* invasion episode has been considered previously. Alan

Deyermond described the invasion episode as a "separate and spontaneous reaction to the French poems" (183). Juan Victorio rejected the notion that the invasion episode could be a revival of the Bernardo del Carpio narrative, citing the few parallels between them. Instead, he argued for the episode to be understood in the context of the fratricidal wars between King Pedro I of Castile and his half-brother Enrique of Trastámara in the mid-fourteenth century. In this formulation, the author of the *Mocedades* sided with King Pedro (*petrista*) against Enrique and his French allies, and his implacable Francophobia inspired the invasion episode, making the narrative a "texto antifrancés." Victorio's compositional theory has been largely discredited, perhaps most forcefully by Fernando Gómez Redondo (139–40). Vaquero considers a common sociopolitical background and similar geographical landscapes in the two narratives as sufficient evidence to support an argument for influence (128).

28 In a few instances the English translations of the *Mocedades* differ slightly from the published text.

29 Prof. Mariane Ailes, an expert on the French *chanson de geste*, recognized this parallel in response to a presentation I made at the University of Bristol in the spring of 2012.

30 The extraordinary popularity of the subject matter of *Fierabras* is attested in the sixteen extant manuscripts transcribed across three centuries (thirteenth to fifteenth), in six different French dialects and located in six countries, including Spain (Newth xxvi). The most influential of all the adaptations of *Fierabras* was that of Jehan Bagnyon (1478), translated into Spanish in 1521 by Nicolás de Piamonte, including the confrontation cited above: "O Emperador Carlo Magno, hombre cobarde y sin ninguna virtud, envia dos, tres, o cuatro de los mejores de tus varones a un hombre solo que espera batalla, aunque sea Roldan, Oliveros, Tierri, Oger de Danois, que te juro a mis dioses no les volver la cara, aunque sean seis, cata que estoy en el campo solo, y muy alejado de los mios; y si esto no haces, por todo el mundo publicaré tu cobardía y la de los tuyos, indignos de se llamar Caballeros" (Piamonte 23).

2 Affect and the Quest for Narrative Coherence

1 This chapter represents a substantial revision of an earlier publication ("Affective Response").

2 Montgomery's compiler is not the copyist, a later hand who first attempted to render the narrative in prose before conceding its poetic essence (Gómez Redondo 138–9), and was intent on clarifying genealogical connections and historical details (Montgomery, "The Lengthened Lines" esp. 4–5, 12).

3 Lacomba published her article the same year as I published my findings on the narrative cohesion of the *Mocedades* ("Affective Response"), so there is no cross-referencing. However, my more general earlier formulations on narrative coherence in the poem were available (Introduction 11–14) and reviewed (Martín).

4 Montgomery's notion of a compiler has relevance for this conception of the poem's author, in that much of its content existed prior to its composition as the *Mocedades* ("Las *MR* y los romances" 132–3). However, as the present argument intends, the author is more than a compiler, as the composition is guided by a unifying theme and an aesthetic coherence that inform the selection of the specific traditional material that constitute the poem.

5 A plausible resolution to the question of the poem's ending is proposed by David Hook and Antonia Long.

6 J. Enrique Serrano Asenjo sees a positive progression in the portrayal of Rodrigo's rite of passage, with favourable attributes identified in his relationship with King Fernando, and in his acts of charity. This progression leads him to rise above the human condition to an ineffable status "más allá del bien y del mal" ["beyond good and evil"] (165). Lacomba also sees Rodrigo's exemplarity in the three encounters that Funes had identified as "dominado por la oposición entre una figura de rebeldía y una figura de autoridad" ["characterized by the opposition between a rebellious figure and an authority figure"] (para. 4).

7 Rodrigo's first challenge to his father's authority is only suggested. As Diego Laínez has gathered his family and vassals to do battle against Count don Gómez de Gormaz, Ximena's father, the poem notes that Rodrigo, "Cuéntasse en los çien lidiadores, que quisso el padre o que non" ["He is counted among the one hundred warriors, whether his father wanted it or not"] (v. 373).

8 The term and its use in ancient Greek literature are explored in six lectures delivered in English by Michel Foucault at UC Berkeley in the fall term of 1983. The lectures were recorded and later compiled and published as *Fearless Speech* in 2001. Foucault died in 1984.

9 In a previous iteration of this chapter, I had described Rodrigo as speaking truth to power with no reference to Foucault. An anonymous reviewer indicated the relevance of Foucault's work to my analysis, which led me to incorporate references to his work and in so doing expand and broaden the analysis.

10 In the case of Chaucer, Paul Megna suggests that the author was interested in using *parrhesia* "in an effort to (re)build the actual world in which he lived" (32), while the monarch being addressed was the despotic Richard II (39).

11 Montgomery applies the term "femme impudique" to Ximena because he (and presumably the audience of the work) considers that she should still

be in mourning for her father's death when she boldly asks King Fernando for Rodrigo's hand in marriage, the very man who had killed him. This marriage is advantageous to Ximena for material reasons, expressed clearly in the *CC*, "ca só çierta que la su fazienda ha de seer en el mayor estado de ningún omne del vuestro señorío" ["for I am certain that his estate will be greater than that of any man in all your lands"] ("Fernando I el Magno" para. 15; chap. 3), as well as emotionally in the *MR*, "Ella tendió los ojos e a Rodrigo comenzó de catarlo,/dixo, 'Señor, muchas merçedes, ca éste es el conde que yo demando'" ["She raised her eyes and looked Rodrigo over,/saying, 'Sire, I am very grateful, this is the count that I desire'"] (vv. 488–9), attributing to Rodrigo a rank he does not have. Even so, Montaner views this attribution of impropriety to Ximena as "gratuito" ["gratuitous"] since "nada prohibía a una mujer medieval pedir justicia ante un atropello" ["nothing prohibited a medieval women from seeking justice after being harmed"] ("Las quejas" 480).
12 In contrast with the standard critical view of the poem, here echoed by Funes who, in speaking broadly of the work, states: "De toda ello resulta una línea ideológica fundamental, orientada a la celebración de la rebeldía" (xlviii).
13 This episode is examined in detail in chap. 4 from another critical perspective.
14 Recall here that the *Crónica de Alfonso X* tends to portray its subject in a negative light, since it was composed in the reign of his great grandson Alfonso XI to serve as a contrast to the latter's more successful reign (Bergqvist 81).
15 Pero Mudo is the nickname of Pero Bermudo, or Bermúdez as in the *Cantar de mio Cid*. It is a play on his difficulty in speaking as a stutterer ("tartamudo"), rendering him mute ("mudo"), as it were.

3 Chronicle Prose and Rodrigo's Epic Deeds

 1 The traditional date of composition for the *Crónica de Castilla* is in the early years of the reign of King Fernando IV, as in Carlos Alvar and Juan Bautista Crespo, who cite Luis Filipe Lindley Cintra and Diego Catalán as authorities on the dating of the *CC* between 1295 and 1312 (285). Samuel Armistead dates the composition of the *CC* as "circa 1300" ("La 'furia guerrera'" 69), or "entre 1290 y 1300" ("La *Crónica de Castilla*" 40), the latter also in Manuel Hijano (645). Patricia Rochwert-Zuili offers a well-reasoned argument for a more specific dating between 1300 and 1301 (para. 30). A succinct review of scholarship on the dating of the *mocedades* narrative, the extant *Mocedades* text, and its relationship to the chronicle text can be found in Matthew Bailey (Introduction 5–8).

2 For a thorough review and analysis of the main points and protagonists
   of this scholarly discussion, made in the course of substantiating his own
   perspective, see Montaner, "La *Gesta*" and "Rodrigo y el gafo" esp. 121–39.
3 This conception of adaptation is echoed in Julie Sanders, with abundant
   theoretical support (20, 25, 41).
4 The date is not in contention and can be referenced in Catalán "con
   anterioridad a 1270" ("Poesía y novella" 426) and Mariano de la Campa
   "hacia el año 1270" (62). See also Brian Powell for an end date of 1274 (35).
5 These distinct periods are (1) early Spanish history before the Goths, (2) history
   of the Gothic kings, (3) kings of León from Pelayo to Vermudo III, (4) kings of
   Castile and León from Fernando I to Fernando III (Fernández Ordóñez 11–12).
6 Also, in other words, "El segmento dedicado a los reyes de Castilla …
   solo nos ha llegado a través de una serie de formaciones cronísticas que
   reelaboraron de diversas formas el texto original, el cual probablemente
   nunca pasó de un estado de borrador" (Hijano 647).
7 Armistead reviews the references to the young Rodrigo in the *CVR* and
   concludes that although they are scant, they will resurface later in a more
   elaborate fashion and thus reflect an evolving narrative on the youth
   of Rodrigo ("Las primeras alusiones" 34–9). Catalán rationalizes his
   disagreement with Armistead's conjecture (*El Cid en la historia* 236–8). For
   a review of the relevant scholarship, see Montaner, "La *Gesta*" esp. 431–2,
   and note 4, also 433–4.
8 I cite Hijano on the relationship between the various predecessors to the
   Crónica de Castilla because his article provides a succinct and exceptionally
   clear review of the otherwise incredibly detailed and intricate scholarship
   on the subject produced over the course of more than a century.
   Previous scholarship is frustratingly difficult to document and follow,
   in part because it was constantly being revised and because most of the
   manuscripts cited are unpublished and thus unavailable for verification. A
   similar synopsis is eloquently formulated in David Pattison (*From Legend
   to Chronicle* 3–4).
9 Pattison aptly describes the *CC* as "distinguished by its uncritical use of
   popular sources and by a very marked tendency to elaborate narrative
   details, dialogue, and description" (*From Legend to Chronicle* 6).
10 Armistead reviews a similar trajectory for the Cidian material in the *CC*
   ("La *Crónica de Castilla*" 43–4).
11 Following similar reasoning, Armistead refers to the *CC* as "un texto
   crucial, una piedra clave de la historiografía neo-Alfonsí" ("La *Crónica de
   Castilla*" 44). Likewise, Rochwert-Zuili, on the cover of her online edition
   of the *CC* credits its legacy to "(el) lugar que ocupa en el texto el relato
   de la vida del personaje que fue y sigue siendo el único héroe de Castilla:
   Rodrigo Díaz de Vivar, llamado el Cid" ["(the) place occupied by the story

of the life of the character who was and continues to be the lone hero of Castile: Rodrigo Díaz de Vivar, called the Cid"].

12 All references to the *CC* and its content revert to its online edition by Patricia Rochwert-Zuili, based on ms. Esp. 12 of the Bibliothèque Nationale de France with corrections from ms. X-I-11 of the Biblioteca del Escorial. As noted earlier, Ms. Esp. 12 also contains the unique ms. of the *Mocedades*, which has been reproduced in toto from slides of the original in Bailey, ed., between pages 182 and 183. Rochwert-Zuili also reproduces folios 187v–88r of the manuscript, the meeting point of the *CC* and the *Mocedades* (para. 130).

13 Scholars have argued for and against the brief reference in the *PCG* to the knighting of Rodrigo as evidence for the existence of a Rodrigo narrative at the time of its composition (Catalán, *El Cid en la historia* 236–9; Armistead, "Las primeras alusiones" 32–7).

14 The passage that reads "Et fízole el rrey … los otros lugares" is a rephrasing of the original used here for clarification, following Catalán (*El Cid en la historia* 240). "Noueles" is an optional reading for "nobles" (*CC*, "Fernando I el Magno" para. 68n79; chap. 14).

15 This episode also occurs in the *CC*, with some differences. Fernando leaves the administration of justice to Rodrigo so that he may sojourn to Santiago, but the pilgrimage is the king's idea, not suggested by Rodrigo ("Fernando I el Magno" para. 41; chap. 9).

16 Montaner asserts that a putative previous version of the *MR* was indeed the source for the knighting episode in the *CC* (for him, the *Crónica Particular del Cid*, a later version of the *CC*) ("La *Gesta*" 438).

17 Also confirmed in Catalán (*El Cid en la historia* 242).

18 Jesús Rodríguez Velasco has examined the knighting of Rodrigo in several texts, including the *CC* and the *MR*. His argument reinforces the assumption that knighting is associated with actions on the battlefield, "la investidura caballeresca ha de producirse en un acto de valoración heroica, en un hecho guerrero, por ejemplo" (386).

19 See the previous chapters and earlier (Bailey, Introduction 11–14. See also Martín.)

20 This description of the portrayal of Rodrigo in the *CC* is complementary to the more detailed and politically focused portrayal offered by Rochwert-Zuili in her introductory study (paras. 32–86).

4 Holy Warriors: Rodrigo Díaz and His Celestial Champions

1 Montaner also allows for a connection ("Rodrigo y el gafo" 137), but focuses more on other critical matters, such as whether the chronicle version or the epic poem is truer to its source (139). Montgomery reviews this connection and others between the *Táin* and the *MR* (*Medieval Spanish Epic* 29–41).

2 Interest in this episode during the modern era is exemplified in a young-adult novel from pre-Franco-era Spain in which Rodrigo's opponent represents "unsportsman-like behavior" vs. Rodrigo's "masculine physicality and appropriate behavior," reflecting a focus on character (the "moral weakness" of Rodrigo's challenger) as opposed to the spiritual weakness of his Muslim foe in the medieval period (Beck, "Visualizing the Cid" 11).

3 Both terms and their Counter-Reformation significance are analysed in Russell Sebold.

4 Relevant insights include Deyermond 110–15, Armistead ("La 'furia guerrera'" esp. 71–2), and Montaner ("Rodrigo y el gafo" esp. 124–7), who rationalize the episode through the literature and ethos of the period but do not question the intervention of Saint Lazarus in Rodrigo's pilgrimage to the shrine of Saint James.

5 For the dating and textual history of the *Crónica particular del Cid*, see José María Viña Liste v–viii. José Manuel Lucía Megías gives a detailed editorial history of the *Crónica particular* and of the *Crónica popular del Cid* with reproductions of their engravings ("Las dos caras").

6 Anecdotally, the Wikipedia entry for the Iglesia de San Lázaro (Palencia), states that tradition dates the construction of the church to 1076, to a property founded by the Cid, that served as a hospital (residence) for pilgrims and lepers, as recorded in an inscription above the door: "La tradición adjudica la erección de esta iglesia en 1076 en un inmueble fundado por el Cid Campeador que funcionaba como hospital de peregrinos y leprosos, tal como recuerda una inscripción sobre la puerta."

7 Montaner reviews the identification of the site of the encounter in the poem ("Rodrigo y el gafo" 137n65).

8 Montaner does find a functional correspondence between the promise of Saint Lazarus to Rodrigo and the promise of Saint Gabriel to the mature Cid at the very outset of his exile, an episode included much later in the chronicle, but of course not part of the *MR*, limited to the deeds of the young Cid. In this conception, the promise of divine support is given to Rodrigo as he sets out to make himself into a man worthy of marriage, and to the mature Cid as he sets out in his quest to regain his lost honour (Montaner, "Rodrigo y el gafo" 125).

9 Deyermond provides an early introduction to the critical conception of the now-lost *Gesta* (9–15).

10 Montaner and Ángel Escobar review the episode in detail (17–26).

11 The divine nature of the breath of Saint Lazarus is reviewed by Montaner in the context of the previous studies by Montgomery and Armistead (Montaner, "Rodrigo y el gafo" 126–9). Giles details its Christian-centric context and meaning with reference to the findings of Armistead (esp. 18 and note 6).

12 There is one additional episode in the *MR* in which Rodrigo's Christian charity is on display (vv. 545–6).

5 Guillén de Castro's *Mocedades del Cid* and the Traditional Ballad

1 Succinctly, and in other words, in the *MC* "se armoniza la coherencia ideológica del sistema con la coherencia ideológica del producto. El teatro, en términos de Althusser, como Aparato Ideológico de Estado" ["the ideological coherence of the system is harmonized with the ideological coherence of the product. Theatre, in the words of Althusser, as Ideological Apparatus of the State"] (Ramos 74).
2 Stephano Arata reviews these characterizations in a single paragraph (xlviii).
3 Lauren Beck notes the novelty of the inclusion of "the illustrated typologies of soldier" in Escobar's volume (*Illustrating the Cid* 270).
4 Escobar's collection remained the principal poetic biography of the Cid until the nineteenth century (Egido, Estudio preliminar xii).
5 These luminaries include "desde Voltaire a Victor Hugo, desde Schlegel a Sainte-Beuve" ["from Voltaire a Victor Hugo, from Schlegel a Sainte-Beuve"] (Arata lxxii).
6 The review of the fortunes of Guillén's play follows Arata xxxi, xliv–xlv, xlviii, lxv, lxxi, lxxiv–lxxv.
7 Françoise Cazal confirms that the written sources used by Guillén were two specific ballad texts, *Romancero general* (1600) and *Historia y romancero del Cid* (1605), imagining "cuando Guillén trabajaba sobre unos romances precisos, disponía de ellos en una forma escrita, en su mesa de trabajo" ["when Guillén worked with specific ballads, they were available to him in written form, on his desk"] (97).
8 The subjects of the unique engravings incorporated into the text of the *Crónica popular del Cid* suggest that its readers were most interested in the deeds of the mature Cid (Lucía Megías, "Leer el *Cid*" 414–16, also "Las dos caras" 724–33). This is clearly not the case with Guillén and his imagined audience or the Cidian ballad tradition ("romances tradicionales").
9 In reference to the epic text and the *CC* (as well as the later *Crónica de 1344*) Arata assures us that "todos estos testimonios ofrecen una version muy similar de la leyenda" ["All these testimonies offer a very similar version of the legend"] (xxxviii). An indirect refutation of that statement is the analysis offered in chap. 3.
10 The chronicle text of the reign of Fernando I prior to the incorporation of the material on Rodrigo's youth (previous to the *CC*) is found in the *Primera crónica general o sea Estoria de España* (*PCG*), composed under the auspices of Alfonso X. More details and citations are offered in chap. 3.

11 In the play, the father of Ximena is el Conde Lozano or el Conde de Orgaz.
    In the medieval tradition, he is el Conde don Gómez de Gormaz. Here he
    will be referred to as "el Conde."

12 Cazal identifies five ballads that are substantially incorporated into the
    play. Of these, only two involve Rodrigo, while the remaining three depict
    Ximena's pleas for justice (121).

13 Arata reviews some of the scholarship on the introduction of the love
    interest between Rodrigo and Ximena at the outset of Guillén's play. He
    considers it the most important innovation in the narration of Rodrigo's
    youthful deeds (lxi).

14 Cazal is in agreement with Arata's assessment of the role of the ballads,
    but her more rigorous standard for what constitutes the incorporation
    of a ballad leads her to reduce Arata's twelve ballads to five, "una
    comedia que inserta cinco romances" ["a comedy that inserts five
    ballads"] (96).

15 Arata maintains that Ximena's contrastive portrayal was present in
    the ballads and that Guillén was able to accommodate it within the
    conventional female characteristic of the Baroque drama ["los rasgos
    tipológicos de la dama de la comedia"]: "que esconde su amor detrás de
    una actitud recatada y discreta, que confía su pasión solo al secreto de los
    apartes, que vive con resignación la imposibilidad de su amor" ["who
    hides her love behind a discreet and shy attitude, who confines her passion
    to the secrecy of the asides, and who resigns herself to the impossibility of
    her love"], and the virile ["viril"] female characters of sixteenth-century
    drama (lxiii). Ballads may have portrayed Ximena in more than one
    fashion, but the three that Guillén incorporated all focus on her justice-
    seeking self.

16 For insight into Guillén's decision to proceed in this fashion, we might
    look to Ben Jonson's *Sejanus* (1605), another playwright of the time who
    wrote historical dramas based on earlier sources, but also found a way to
    make the historical material relevant to a contemporary audience. Jonson's
    contributions to the play speak to the world of his audience and in
    combination with the intrigue of his sources, create passages that "might
    have made James I and prominent courtiers distinctly uncomfortable"
    (Goldfarb 60).

17 The stalking is clearly expressed, while the sexual aggression is expressed
    metaphorically through Rodrigo's baiting of his hawk in Ximena's
    dovecote ("palomar"), which stains her apron with blood. Critics have
    delved into the various manifestations of this imagery for its meaning, a
    process reviewed and supported by Alison Carberry (47–53). Carol Evans
    interprets the metaphorical imagery somewhat loosely as Rodrigo's rape
    of Ximena (67–9), also reported from other sources in Montaner ("Las

quejas" 483–4), who sees in the imagery a subconscious sexual desire on the part of Ximena (487).

18 Ximena is grotesque in the sense of an unruly woman (Russo 58). Her appearance is unruly, "desmelenado el cabello/llorando a su padre el Conde" ['her hair disheveled/crying over her father the Count"] (Escobar 130), as it mirrors her engagement in an extreme act of defiance of the public order, a female transgressor acting out a kind of public spectacle, following Mary Russo (61). This behaviour is of course portrayed in the play as out of character for Ximena, and as such, will be reconciled by a return to her compliant self.

19 Foucault makes the useful distinction between political and personal *parrhesia*, through the examples of Ion's generic critique of the monarchy (political) and his mother's truthful accusation against Apollo, her rapist (56).

20 The silencing of the medieval Rodrigo and Ximena, even though through diverse means, does not seem to match the kind of gender differentiation that Lynda Boose finds in her study of sixteenth- and early seventeenth-century England (189).

Works Cited

Agheana, Ion T. "Guillén de Castro's Jimena: An Exemplary Character and Its Flaw." *Bulletin of the Comediantes*, vol. 29, no. 1, 1977, pp. 34–8.

Ahern, Stephen. "Nothing More Than Feelings? Affect Theory Reads the Age of Sensibility." *The Eighteenth Century: Theory and Interpretation*, vol. 58, no. 3, 2017, pp. 281–95.

Alonso, Dámaso. "La primitive épica francesa a la luz de una *Nota Emilianense*." *Revista de Filología Española*, vol. 37, 1953, pp. 1–94.

Alvar, Carlos, and Juan Bautista Crespo. "*Crónica de Castilla*." *Diccionario filológico de literature medieval española. Textos y transmisión*, edited by Alvar and José Manule Lucía Megías, Castalia, 2002, pp. 285–92.

Alvar, Carlos et al., editors. *El Cid: De la material épica a las crónicas caballerescas. Actas del Congreso Internacional "IX Centenario de la muerte del Cid."* Alcalá UP, 2002.

Arata, Stefano. Prólogo. *Las mocedades del Cid*, by Guillén de Castro, Crítica, 1996, pp. xxxi–lxxxii.

Armistead, Samuel G. "Las primeras alusiones a las *Mocedades de Rodrigo*." *La tradición épica de las "Mocedades de Rodrigo,"* by Armistead, Salamanca UP, 1974, pp. 31–7.

– "La 'furia guerrera' en dos textos épicos." *La tradición épica de las "Mocedades de Rodrigo,"* by Armistead. Salamanca UP, 1987, pp. 69–77.

– "La *Crónica de Castilla* y las *Mocedades*." *La tradición épica de las "Mocedades de Rodrigo,"* by Armistead, Salamanca UP, 1997, pp. 39–48.

– *La tradición épica de las "Mocedades de Rodrigo."* Salamanca UP, 2000.

Bailey, Matthew. *The Transformation of an Epic Tradition: The "Poema del Cid" and the "Poema de Fernán González."* Hispanic Seminary of Medieval Studies, 1993.

–, editor. *Las "Mocedades de Rodrigo": Estudios críticos, manuscrito y edición.* King's College Centre for Late Antique and Medieval Studies, 1999.

- Introduction. *Las Mocedades de Rodrigo/The Youthful Deeds of the Rodrigo, the Cid*, edited and translated by Bailey. U of Toronto P, 2007, pp. 3–27.
- *The Poetics of Speech in the Medieval Spanish Epic*. U of Toronto P, 2010.
- "Charlemagne as a Creative Force in the Spanish Epic." *Charlemagne and His Legend in Early Spanish Literature and Historiography*, edited by Bailey and Ryan Giles. U of Toronto P, 2016, pp. 13–43.
- "Affective Response and Narrative Coherence in the *Mocedades de Rodrigo*." *Romance Quarterly*, vol. 66, no. 3, 2019, pp. 124–34.
Bailey, Matthew, and Ryan Giles, editors. *Charlemagne and His Legend in Early Spanish Literature and Historiography*. U of Toronto P, 2016.
Barton, Simon, and Richard Fletcher, editors and translators. *The World of El Cid: Chronicles of the Spanish Reconquest*. Manchester UP, 2000.
Bautista, Francisco. "Memoria de Carlomagno: Sobre la difusión temprana de la material carolingia en España (siglos XI–XII)." *Revista de Poética Medieval*, vol. 25, 2011, pp. 47–109.
Beck, Lauren. "Visualizing the Cid and His Enemies in Print: The Matamoros Effect." *Image & Narrative*, vol. 17, no. 1, 2016, pp. 5–14.
- *Illustrating the Cid, 1498 to Today*. McGill-Queen's UP, 2019.
Bennett, Philip E. "Origins of the French Epic: The *Song of Roland* and Other French Epics." *Approaches to Teaching the "Song of Roland"*, edited by William W. Kibler and Leslie Zarker Morgan. Modern Language Association of America, 2006, pp. 57–65.
Berganza, Francisco de. *Antigüedades de España propugnadas en las noticias de sus reyes, y condes de Castilla la Vieja: En la historia apologética de Rodrigo de Bivar, dicho el Cid Campeador y en la corónica del Real Monasterio de San Pedro de Cardeña. Parte Primera*. Francisco del Hierro, 1719.
Bergqvist, Kim. "Tears of Weakness, Tears of Love: Kings as Fathers and Sons in Medieval Spanish Prose." *Tears, Sighs and Laughter: Expression of Emotions in the Middle Ages*, edited by Per Fornegård et al. Kungl. Vitterhets Historie och Antikvitets Akademien, 2017, pp. 77–97.
Boose, Lynda E. "Scolding Brides and Bridling Scolds: Taming the Woman's Unruly Member." *Shakespeare Quarterly*, vol. 42, no. 2, 1991, pp. 179–213.
Campa, Mariano de la. "La *Versión primitiva* de la *Estoria de España* de Alfonso X: Edición crítica." *Actas del XIII Congreso de la Asociación Internacional de Hispanistas*, edited by Florencio Sevilla y Carlos Alvar, vol. 1. Castalia, 2000, pp. 59–72.
Cantar de mio Cid. Edited by Alberto Montaner. Crítica, 1993.
Carberry, Alison D. "Subverted Tradition and Emotional Impact: Female Characterization in the Epic and *Romancero Viejo*." Dissertation, Boston UP, 2013.
Carmen Campidoctoris. Edited by Juan Gil. Brepols, 1990, pp. 99–108. Chronica Hispana saecvlo XII. Pars I.

Carson, Ciaran, translator. *The Táin: A New Translation of the "Táin Bó Cúailnge"*. Viking, 2008.

Castigos del rey Sancho IV. Edited by Hugo Oscar Bizzarri. Iberoamericana, 2001.

Castro, Guillén de. *Las mocedades del Cid-Comedia segunda*. Edited by María Edmée Álvarez, Porrúa, 1985.

— *Las mocedades del Cid*. Edited by Stefano Arata. Crítica, 1996.

Catalán, Diego. "Poesía y novela en la historiografía castellana de los siglos xiii–xiv." *Mèlanges Offerts à Rita Lejeune, professeur à l'Université d'Liège*, edited by Rita Lejeune, vol. 1, Editions J. Ducolot, 1969, pp. 423–41.

— *El Cid en la historia y sus inventores*. Fundación Menéndez Pidal, 2002.

Cazal, Françoise. "Romancero y reescritura dramática: Las mocedades del Cid." *Criticón*, vol. 72, 1998, pp. 93–123.

Chalon, Louis. "L'histoire de la monarchie asturienne, de Pelayo à Alphonse II le Chaste, dans le *Poema de Fernán González*." *Marche Romane*, vol. 20, no. 1, 1970, pp. 61–7.

Christensen, Hannah M. "Affect and the Limits of Form in *Sir Amadace*." *Exemplaria*, vol. 29, no. 2, 2017, pp. 99–117.

Corneille, Pierre. *Le Cid*. Translated by Vincent J. Cheng, Delaware UP, 1987.

Crapotta, James, and Marcia L. Welles. Introduction. *Las mocedades del Cid*, edited by Crapotta and Welles. Cervantes & Co., 2002, pp. 7–16.

Crónica de Castilla. Edited by Patricia Rochwert-Zuili. SEMH-Sorbonne - CLEA, EA 4083, 2010, journals.openedition.org/e-spanialivres/256. Accessed 7 June 2018.

Deyermond, A. D. *Epic Poetry and the Clergy: Studies on the "Mocedades de Rodrigo."* Tamesis, 1969.

Díaz-Mas, Paloma. *Romancero*. Crítica, 1994.

Duggan, Joseph J. "Beyond the Oxford Text: The Songs of Roland." *Approaches to Teaching the "Song of Roland,"* edited by William W. Kibler and Leslie Zarker Morgan. MLA, 2006, pp. 66–72.

Egido, Aurora. "Mito, géneros y estilos: El Cid barroco." *Boletín de la Real Academia Española*, vol. 59, no. 218, 1979, pp. 499–528.

— Estudio Preliminar. *Las mocedades del Cid*, by Guillén de Castro. Crítica, 1996, pp. ix–xxvii.

Einhard. *Vita Karoli Magni: The Life of Charlemagne*. Edited and translated by Evelyn Scherabon Firchow and Edwin H. Zeydel, U of Miami P, 1972.

Ellul, Max J. *The Sword and the Green Cross: The Saga of the Knights of Saint Lazarus from the Crusades to the 21st Century*. Author House, 2011.

Escobar, Juan de, editor. *Historia y romancero del Cid*.1605, Castalia, 1973.

Evans, Carol Anne. "The Plea of a Woman: Las quejas de Jimena." *Romance Notes*, vol. 38, no. 1, 1997, pp. 61–70.

Faliu-Lacourt, Christiane. *Un dramaturge espagnol du Siècle d'Or: Guillén de Castro*. Université-Le Mirial, 1989.

Falque Rey, E. Introducción. *Historia Roderici*, Brepols, 1990, pp. 1–43. Chronica Hispana saecvli XII. Pars I.

Fernández del Pulgar, Pedro. *Teatro clerical, apostólico, y secvlar, de las Iglesias de España, primera parte, libro segvndo*. Nieto, 1680.

Fernández Ordóñez, Inés. Estudio. *Versión critica de la Estoria de España*, Seminario Menéndez Pidal, 1993, pp. 9–352.

Fernández Valverde, Juan. Introducción. *Historia de rebus Hispanie sive Historia Gothica*, by Rodrigo Jiménez de Rada. Brepols, 1987, pp. 9–47.

Fierabras. *Chanson de geste*. Edited by A. Kroeber and G. Servois. 1860, Kraus Reprint Corporation, 1966.

Fierabras and Floripas: A French Epic Allegory. Edited and translated by Michael A. H. Newth. Italica, 2010.

Foucault, Michel. *Fearless Speech*. Edited by Joseph Pearson. Semiotext(e), 2001.

Fradejas Lebrero, José. "Valores literarios de la *Crónica de veinte reyes*." *Crónica de veinte reyes*, edited by César Hernández Alonso et al. Ayuntamiento de Burgos, 1991, pp. 31–51.

Funes, Leonardo. Estudio. *Mocedades de Rodrigo: Estudio y edición de los tres estados del texto*, edited by Funes con Felipe Tannenbaum. Tamesis, 2004, pp. ix–lxxii.

Gil, Juan. Introducción. *Carmen Campidoctoris*, Brepols, 1990, pp. 101–2. Chronica Hispana saecvlo XII, Pars. I.

Giles, Ryan D. "The Breath of Lazarus in the *Mocedades de Rodrigo*." *Beyond Sight: Engaging the Senses in Iberian Literatures and Cultures: 1200–1750*, edited by Giles and Steven Wagschall. U of Toronto P, 2018, pp. 17–30.

Goldfarb, Philip. "Jonson's Renaissance Romans: Classical Adaptation in *Sejanus*." *Interdiscplinary Humanities*, vol. 31, no. 3, 2014, pp. 53–62.

Gómez Redondo, Fernando. "Las *Mocedades* cronísticas." *Las "Mocedades de Rodrigo": Estudios críticos, manuscrito y edición*, edited by Matthew Bailey. King's College Centre for Late Antique and Medieval Studies, 1999, pp. 137–61.

Hazbun, Geraldine. *Narratives of the Islamic Conquests from Medieval Spain*. Palgrave Macmillan, 2015.

Hijano, Manuel. "La *Crónica de Castilla*: Tradición e innovación." *Literatura medieval y renacentista en España: Líneas y pautas*, edited by Natalia Fernández Rodríguez and María Fernández Ferreiro. Sociedad de Estudios Medievales y Renacentistas, 2012, pp. 643–54.

Historia Roderici. Edited by E. Falque Rey. Brepols, 1990, pp. 45–98. Chronica Hispana saecvli XII, Pars I.

Historia Silensis. Edited by Juan A. Estévez Sola. Brepols, 2018.

Hook, David, and Antonia Long. "Reflexiones sobre la estructura de las *Mocedades de Rodrigo*." *Las "Mocedades de Rodrigo": Estudios críticos, manuscrito y edición*, edited by Matthew Bailey. King's College Centre for Late Antique and Medieval Studies, 1999, pp. 53–67.

"Iglesia de San Lázaro (Palencia)." *Wikipedia*, es.wikipedia.org/wiki/Iglesia _de_San_Lázaro_(Palencia). Accessed 18 July 2019.

Jiménez de Rada, Rodrigo. *Historia de rebus Hispanie sive Historia Gothica*. Edited by Juan Fernández Valverde. Brepols, 1987.

Kibler, William W., and Leslie Zarker Morgan, editors. *Approaches to Teaching the "Song of Roland."* MLA, 2006.

Lacarra Lanz, Eukene. "Political Discourse and the Construction and Representation of Gender in *Mocedades de Rodrigo*." *Hispanic Review*, vol. 67, no. 4, 1999, pp. 467–91.

Lacomba, Marta. "El héroe y la verdad: El valor demostrativo de la analogía narrativa en las *Mocedades de Rodrigo*." *e-Spania*, no. 34, outubre 2019, doi:10.4000/e-spania.32233. Accessed 17 January 2023.

Las Mocedades de Rodrigo/The Youthful Deeds of Rodrigo, the Cid. Edited and translated by Matthew Bailey. U Toronto P, 2007.

Latowsky, Anne A. *Emperor of the World: Charlemagne and the Construction of Imperial Authority, 800–1229*. Cornell UP, 2013.

Lewis, David Levering. *God's Crucible: Islam and the Making of Europe, 570–1215*. W.W. Norton, 2008.

Leys, Ruth. "The Turn to Affect: A Critique." *Critical Inquiry*, vol. 37, no. 3, 2011, pp. 434–72.

Libro de Fernán González. Edited by Itzíar López Guil. CSIC, 2001.

Lindley Cintra, Luís Filipe, editor. *Crónica geral de Espanha de 1344*, vol. 1. Imprensa Nacional-Casa da Moeda, 1951.

Linehan, Peter. "Fechas y sospechas sobre Lucas de Tuy." *Anuario de Estudios Medievales*, vol. 32, no. 1, 2002, pp. 19–38.

Lorenzo, Ramón. "La interconexión de Castilla, Galicia y Portugal en la confección de las crónicas medievales y en la transmission de textos literarios." *Revista de filología románica*, vol. 19, 2002, pp. 93–123.

Lucía Megías, José Manuel. "Las dos caras de un héroe." *L'Épopée Romane au Moyen Áge et aux Temps Modernes. Actes du XIV° Congrès International de la Société Rencesvals pour l'Étude des Épopées Romanes*, edited by Salvatore Luongo, 2001, pp. 704–36.

– "Leer el *Cid* en el siglo XVI." *El Cid: de la materia épica a las crónicas caballerescas: Actas del Congreso Internacional "IX Centenario de la Muerte del Cid,"* edited by Carlos Alvar et al. Universidad de Alcalá, 2002, pp. 407–21.

Marcombe, David. *Leper Knights: The Order of St. Lazarus of Jerusalem in England, c. 1150–1544*. Boydell, 2003.

Martin, Georges. *Review of Historia Silensis, Corpvs Christianorvm, Continuatio mediaeualis, LXXI B*. Edited by Juan A. Estévez Sola, Brepols, 2018, *e-Spania*, journals.openedition.org/e-spania/29433. Accessed 14 January 2023.

Martín, Oscar. "Review of *Las Mocedades de Rodrigo/The Youthful Deeds of Rodrigo, the Cid*, Edited and Translated by Matthew Bailey." *Speculum*, vol. 84, no. 2, 2009, pp. 393–4.

Matulka, Barbara. *The Cid as a Courtly Hero: From the "Amadís" to Corneille.* Columbia UP, Institute of French Studies, 1928.

Megna, Paul. "Chaucerian *Parrhesia:* World-Building and Truth-Telling in *The Canterbury Tales* and 'Lak of Steadfastnesse.'" *Postmedieval: A Journal of Medieval Cultural Studies*, vol. 9, no. 1, 2017, pp. 30–43.

Menéndez Pidal, Ramón. *La España del Cid.* Plutarco, 1929.

Montaner, Alberto. "La **Gesta de las mocedades de Rodrigo* y la *Crónica particular del Cid.*" *Actas del 1 congreso de la Asociación hispánica de literature medieval*, edited by Vicente Beltrán, Barcelona PPU, 1988, pp. 431–44.

– *Política, historia y drama en el "Cerco de Zamora."* Zaragoza UP, 1989.

– "Las quejas de Doña Jimena: formación y desarrollo de un tema en la épica y en el Romancero." *Actas del II Congreso internacional de la Asociación hispánica de literatura medieval*, edited by José Manuel Lucía Mejías et al. Alcalá de Henares UP, 1991, pp. 475–507.

– "Rodrigo y el gafo." *El Cid: De la material épica a las crónicas caballerescas. Actas del Congreso Internacional "IX Centenario de la muerte del Cid,"* edited by Carlos Alvar et al. Alcalá UP, 2002, pp. 121–79.

Montaner, Alberto, and Ángel Escobar, editors. *Carmen Campidoctoris o Poema latino del Campeador.* España Nuevo Milenio, 2001.

Montgomery, Thomas. "Some Singular Passages in the *Mocedades de Rodrigo.*" *Journal of Hispanic Philology*, vol. 7, no. 2, 1983, pp. 121–34.

– "Las *Mocedades de Rodrigo* y los romances." *Josep Maria Sola-Solé: Homage, Homenaje, Homenatge: Miscelánea de estudios de amigos y discíupulos*, edited by Antonio Torres Alcalá, vol. 2. Puvill, 1984, pp. 119–33.

– 'The Lengthened Lines of the *Mocedades de Rodrigo.*" *Romance Philology*, vol. 38, no. 1, 1984, pp. 1–14.

– "Horatius, Cúchulainn, Rodrigo de Vivar." *Revista Canadiense de Estudios Hispánicos*, vol. 11, no. 3, 1987, pp. 541–57.

– *Medieval Spanish Epic: Mythic Roots and Ritual Language.* Penn State UP, 1998.

– "Las *Mocedades de Rodrigo* y el *Táin Bó Cúailnge.*" *Las "Mocedades de Rodrigo": Estudios críticos, manuscrito y edición*, edited by Matthew Bailey. King's College Centre for Late Antique and Medieval Studies, 1999, pp. 37–52.

Newth, Michael A. H. Introduction. *Fierabras and Floripas: A French Epic Allegory*, edited by Newth. Italica, 2010, pp. 9–35.

Order of Saint Lazarus of Jerusalem. *The Sovereign Military and Hospitaller Order of Saint Lazarus of Jerusalem.* Grand Priory of the Western United States of America, 1941.

Pattison, David. *From Legend to Chronicle: The Treatment of Epic Material in Alfonsine Historiography*. Society for the Study of Medieval Languages and Literatures, 1983.

— "El mio Cid del *Poema* y el de las crónicas: evolución de un héroe." *El Cid: De la material épica a las crónicas caballerescas. Actas del Congreso Internacional "IX Centenario de la muerte del Cid,"* edited by Carlos Alvar et al, Alcalá UP, 2002, pp. 23–7.

Pérez de Urbel, Justo and Atilano González de Zorrilla, eds. *Historia Silense*. CSIC, 1959.

Piamonte, Nicolás de, translator. *Historia del Emperador Carlo Magno, en la cual se trata de las grandes proezas y hazañas de los doce pares de Francia, y de como fueron vendidos por el traidor Ganalon; y de la cruda batalla que hubo Oliveros con Fierabras, Rey de Alejandría*. 1512, Imprenta de A. Berdeguer, 1827.

Poema de Fernán González. Edited by H. Salvador Martínez. Espasa-Calpe, 1991.

Powell, Brian. *Epic and Chronicle: The "Poema de mio Cid" and the "Crónica de veinte reyes."* Modern Humanities Research Association, 1983.

Primera crónica general o sea Estoria de España que mandó componer Alfonso el Sabio y se continuaba bajo Sancho IV en 1289. Edited by Ramón Menéndez Pidal. Bailly/Balliére e hijos, 1906.

Pseudo-Turpin. Edited by H. M. Smyser. The Mediaeval Academy of America, 1937.

Ramos, Juan Luis. "Guillén de Castro en el proceso de la comedia barroca." *Cuadernos de filología III. Literatura, Análisis*, vol. 3, 1983, pp. 169–98.

Ratcliffe, Marjorie. "Powerless or Empowered?: Women in Guillén de Castro's *Las mocedades del Cid* and *Las hazañas del Cid*." *Bulletin of the Comediantes*, vol. 44, no. 2, 1992, pp. 261–7.

Robinson Kelly, Molly. *The Hero's Place: Medieval Literary Traditions of Space and Belonging*. Catholic U of America P, 2009.

Rochwert-Zuili, Patricia. Introduction. *Crónica de Castilla*, edited by Rochwert-Zuili. SEMH-Sorbonne-CLEA (EA 4083), 2010, journals.openedition.org /e-spanialivres/137. Accessed 7 June 2018.

Rodríguez Velasco, Jesús D. "El Cid y la investidura caballeresca." *El Cid: De la material épica a las crónicas caballerescas. Actas del Congreso Internacional "IX Centenario de la muerte del Cid."* Alcalá UP, 2002, pp. 383–92.

Romancero General. Edited by Luis Sánchez (a costa de Miguel Martínez), 1600. Facsimile edition printed for Archer M. Huntington, 1904. Kraus Reprint Corporation, 1967.

Royal Frankish Annals (741–829). Carolingian Chronicles: "Royal Frankish Annals" and Nithard's "Histories". Translated by Bernhard Walter Scholz and Barbara Rogers, Michigan UP, 1970, pp. 35–125.

Russo, Mary. *The Female Grotesque: Risk, Excess and Modernity*. Routledge, 1994.

Sanders, Julie. *Adaptation and Appropriation*. Routledge, 2006.

Scherabon Firchow, Evelyn, and Edwin H. Zeydel. Introduction. *Vita Karoli Magni: The Life of Charlemagne*, by Einhard, U of Miami P, 1972, pp. 13–28.

Scholz, Bernhard Walter, and Barbara Rogers. Introduction. *Carolingian Chronicles: "Royal Frankish Annals" and Nithard's "Histories"*, translated by Bernhard Walter Scholz and Marcia L. Welles. U of Michigan P, 1970, pp. 1–33.

Sebold, Russell P. "Un David español, o galán divino, el Cid contrarreformista de Guillén de Castro." *Homage to John M. Hill: In Memoriam*, edited by Walter Poesse et al. Indiana UP, 1968, pp. 217–42.

Serrano Asenjo, J. Enrique. "Aspectos de la organización interior de las *Mocedades de Rodrigo*." *Bulletin of Hispanic Studies*, vol. 73, no. 2, 1996, pp. 159–70.

Sholod, Barton. *Charlemagne in Spain*. Librairie Droz, 1966.

Sicart Giménez, Ángel. "La iconografía de Santiago ecuestre en la Edad Media." *Compostellanum*, vol. 27, no. 1–2, 1982, pp. 11–32.

Smyser, H. M. Introduction. *The Pseudo-Turpin*, edited by Smyser, Mediaeval Academy of America, 1937, pp. 1–11.

Southey, Robert. *Chronicle of the Cid, Rodrigo Diaz de Bivar, el Campeador*. William Pople, 1808.

Tudensis, Lucas. *Chronicon mundi*. Edited by Emma Falque. Brepols, 2003.

Vaquero, Mercedes. "Las *Mocedades de Rodrigo* en el marco de la épica de revuelta Española." *Las "Mocedades de Rodrigo": Estudios críticos, manuscrito y edición*, edited by Matthew Bailey, King's College Centre for Late Antique and Medieval Studies, 1999, pp. 99–136.

Victorio, Juan. "Las *Mocedades de Rodrigo*: Texto Antifrancés." *Charlemagne et l'épopée romane, Actes du VIIe Congrès International de la Société Rencesvals*. Société d'Edition 'Les Belles Lettres,' 1978, pp. 697–705.

Viña Liste, José María. Introducción. *"Crónica del famoso cavallero Cid Ruy Díez Campeador," Mio Cid Campeador: Cantar de mio Cid, Mocedades de Rodrigo, Crónica del famoso caballero*. Biblioteca Castro, 2006, pp. 2–22.

Zamora Vicente, Alonso, editor. *Poema de Fernán González*. Espasa-Calpe, 1946.

Index

Toronto Iberic

Co-editors: Robert Davidson (Toronto) and Frederick A. de Armas (Chicago)

Editorial Board: Josiah Blackmore (Harvard); Marina Brownlee (Princeton); Anthony J. Cascardi (Berkeley); Justin Crumbaugh (Mt. Holyoke); Emily Francomano (Georgetown); Jordana Mendelson (NYU); Joan Ramon Resina (Stanford); Enrique García Santo-Tomás (U Michigan); H. Rosi Song (Durham); Kathleen Vernon (SUNY Stony Brook)

Printed in the USA
CPSIA information can be obtained
at www.ICGtesting.com
JSHW022110220624
65242JS00012B/124/J